MICROPLASTICS AND ME

ANNA DU

For further information, contact:

Tumblehome, Inc.
201 Newbury St, Suite 201
Boston, MA 02116
https://tumblehomebooks.org/

Library of Congress Control Number
2019940379
ISBN-13 978-1-943431-50-2
ISBN-10 1-943431-50-7

Du, Anna
Microplastics and Me / Anna Du - 1st ed

Design: Yu-Yi Ling

10 9 8 7 6 5 4 3 2 1

TUMBLEHOME, INC.,

TUMBLEHOME LEARNING, INC.

MICROPLASTICS AND ME

ANNA DU

CONTENTS

Chapter 1

The Blue Piece Of Plastic That Caught My Eye...

As I turned around, something flashed in the sunlight. It looked like a glimmering jewel. I took a step closer, my bare feet digging into the warm sand, and I knelt down to pick up the best piece of sea glass that I had seen at the beach yet. Though it was smooth to the touch, I could tell it would once have been sharp enough to cut. It was the perfect size, the perfect shape, and the perfect color to make a necklace. It wasn't a dull shade of brown, or a sickly shade of green. Rather, it was a soft, light blue, a color not often found on this beach. Instead of putting it with the other, normal pieces of sea glass, I put it in a smaller pile of my favorites. Then I turned away, looking for more pieces.

My seaglass necklaces

This is what I love about living in New England—it's just not possible to beat the sea glass here. As a self-confessed obsessive "maker," I've always loved making jewelry. Pieces of sea glass are among the best centerpieces for jewelry. They make great gifts for my friends, and they're also environmentally conscious.

Right next to the ocean, I reached for another piece of sea glass. Out of the corner of my eye, I saw my mom trying to signal me, and I turned toward her.

"Watch out—" She didn't get to finish her sentence before a large wave crashed onto my back.

With the cool water soaking through my clothes, I shuddered. My mom shook her head, saying, "I tried to warn you."

Once I came to my senses, I ran to fetch a towel near the tent my dad had set up. As my shivering settled down, I looked around, appreciating the view. Another lazy summer Sunday at the beach. Every week, I came here to pick up sea glass and relax for a few hours. The sea gulls squawked, the waves lapped slowly on the sand, and the warm sea breeze drifted around. I loved how doing absolutely nothing allowed my thoughts to drift and calmed me down as I slowly dried off.

My loyal companion, Andy, came over to lie beside me. I've always seen Andy, who is a German shepherd, as a part of the family. In fact, Andy, or "Andi" in Chinese, means Anna's little brother. I was absent-mindedly rubbing his ears when I

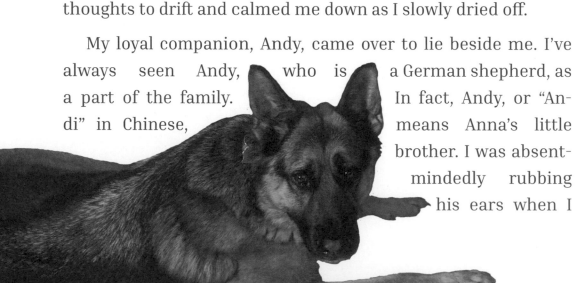

noticed something next to his head, partly covered in sand. It looked like another piece of sea glass. It was an even brighter blue than the piece I'd just collected.

However, as I picked it up and brushed the sand off, it started to feel... wrong. The color was too sharp, too bright, too artificial. It didn't reflect the sun in a way characteristic of glass. It was also way too thin. And it didn't weigh enough for a piece of glass that big. In fact, it didn't feel like sea glass at all. It felt like a piece of plastic.

I scoffed and tossed it aside. For a while, I marched on and continued my mission. However, I kept thinking back to that piece of plastic that I'd tossed aside, and I felt bad. After all, I reasoned with myself, some other sea glass enthusiast in the future might also be fooled by this piece of plastic, and it would be mean for me to just leave it behind. I picked it up and threw it out in the nearest public beach trash barrel. In a weird sort of way, I felt angry at that piece of plastic for making me go through all that effort for nothing. Even when I went back to my collecting, something felt strange. I realized that instead of seeing nature all around me, from rocks to shells to sea glass, I could suddenly only focus on pieces of plastic.

Walking briskly along the shore with Andy at my side, I picked up piece after piece of what looked like sea glass but was actually plastic. Even back at my pile of sea glass, I realized that some of the materials that I'd thought were sea glass... suddenly didn't look a lot like sea glass. Instead, they looked like even more pieces of plastic.

I remembered a video on plastics that my school had shown us weeks before. The video displayed the life cycle of a piece of plastic—from its start in a factory to its end, either in a garbage can or in the ocean. We learned that the amount of plastics that have accumulated in the ocean is so great that there is a floating plastic island called the Great Pacific Garbage Patch, which is larger than Texas. When I watched the school video about this problem, it had seemed so distant. After all, the Pacific Ocean was thousands of miles away. But now, all of a sudden, I could truly see how plastic waste affected me personally.

I wondered why I had never noticed plastics before. Before, if someone had asked me whether there were any pieces of plastic, any pollution on the beach, I would've said no. No way. Now I was starting to see how wrong that statement was. But how could a place which I once thought was full of waves and rocks and sand and exquisite pieces of sea glass so quickly transform into a hulking, ugly heap of pollution in my mind? Where did these plastics come from? Was this how the world truly was? Was it really completely and utterly covered in... plastics?

Chapter 2

Plastics, Plastics Everywhere And Not A Drop You Should Drink

When I got home that day, my eyes were assaulted with the sight of plastics everywhere—the plastic water bottles we used almost daily, the plastic bags just lying there, the pens tossed away without a second thought. It struck me that I would throw most of these objects out after a very short time. Later, after searching plastic facts on the internet, I learned that the average work-life, or the amount of time a plastic item is used, is only around 12 minutes.

Plastics have been around since the early 20th century. Manufacturers favor plastics because they're easy to manipulate. A manufacturer can easily change their chemical composition to emphasize different characteristics—some can be flexible, others stiffer, some light, others heavier, some brittle, others more durable. This is because plastics are long-chain synthetic polymers.

My science teacher once explained to us, "In order to know what polymer means, you need to break the word down. The first part, 'poly,' means many. The whole word means many 'mers', or monomers, or molecules. That is how you know polymers are created out of identical smaller molecules," my teacher said.

Both starch and DNA, which stands for deoxyribonucleic acid, are natural polymers. Starch is made up of long chains of glucose monomers, while DNA consists of repeating nucleotides that transfer information from one generation to the next. Natural polymers are so similar to synthetic polymers in terms of their elemental chemical makeup that at first it's difficult to tell the difference between them. There is one main difference: synthetic polymers don't degrade as easily as natural ones. It can take over five hundred years for a piece of plastic to degrade fully in nature.

As I was researching the use of plastics, I started wondering how plastics are made. What if manufacturing plastics was as harmful to the environment as getting rid of them? I clicked my way to new sites on my computer.

That's when I learned that most plastics are made out of oil and natural gas. Then, through the cracking process, these materials convert into different types of hydrocarbon monomers, with the different combinations forming in different kinds of "nurdles," which are basically plastic beads.

Natural gas is in great demand for energy, so it's very hard to find large deposits of natural gas (also called methane) in easy-to-get pools anymore. The big way people extract natural gas today is by fracking. In fracking, workers inject liquids at high pressures to force open existing cracks in rocks. The rocks fracture, allowing gas workers to extract the natural gas stored within them.

As I read more about fracking, I ran across a story that made me gasp in horror:

So not only was the end product of natural gas—plastics— bad for the environment, the process of attaining the natural gas was also extremely harmful!

A lot of energy is needed to turn the nurdles into plastic products. Extrusion heats up the plastic and moves it through a long, heated cylinder with a revolving screw. In injection molding, the plastics are first heated, then squished into a mold under high pressure.

Once a plastic product finally reaches us, we might use it for a bit—but I learned that the average work-life of a piece of single-use plastic, something made of plastic that we use only once, is only 30 seconds. Then these plastics need to travel to the recycling center, the landfill, or even the ocean.

"Huh. Some of these plastics have traveled to more places than I ever have!" I muttered to myself.

I learned that since the early 20th century, plastics have been used to make more and more everyday products. The number of plastics being used and thrown out has increased so much that in the last twenty years, the amount of plastics produced has been equal to the rest made in history. This surprising statistic does sort of make sense, if you take a look at all the plastics used in our daily lives, from airplanes to a lot of modern medical equipment, to plastic "glasses," to plastic bags, and even to Andy's Frisbee! It seems like nobody can live without plastics in the modern world.

A lot of those plastics end up in the ocean. In the year 2017 alone, 8 million metric tons (a metric ton is 2200 pounds) of plastics were dumped into the sea. It's estimated that by the year 2050, all of the plastics in the ocean, combined, could weigh more than the sea life. Though this number seemed sort of abstract to me—after all, just how heavy is 8 million metric tons? — it did scare me.

What I discovered next was even scarier. The biggest problem is actually quite small. Microplastics are pieces of plastic smaller than 5 millimeters across, many around the size of 10 micrometers, which is 1/100th of a millimeter. That's thinner than a fraction of the thickness of a piece of paper, and smaller than is visible to the human eye! With all of these plastics ending up in the ocean, I began to wonder about plastics in the seafood that we eat.

Microplastics on my finger

I tried to research where the microplastics would be aggregating on the ocean floor. I already knew that scientists could locate the larger pieces of plastics by looking at the Great Pacific Garbage Patch... but what about microplastics? To my dismay, I couldn't find anything relating to where microplastics were aggregating.

I realized that I also *understood* why microplastics weren't being identified—because they were too small. Microplastics are so tiny, people can't see them at all! Besides, microplastics are easily disguised when algae grow on them, or when fish eat them and maybe poop them out.

It seemed to me that even as so much attention is focused on

Synthetic and Natural Plastics

Plastics are made up of organic chemicals known as synthetic polymers, which were discovered in the beginning part of the last century. Polymers are chain-like chemicals made up of repeating smaller structures, made up of organic elements such as C, H, O, N, and others. Sugars and proteins and other molecules which belong to living things are made up of these same "organic" chemicals as well. This similarity can sometimes make it hard to tell synthetic and natural polymers apart without expensive analytical equipment.

Known for their elasticity and toughness, polymers have found many industrial uses over the years. These amazing materials were initially used in products such as nylon stockings and toothbrushes. Now, plastics have become a giant part of our daily lives, used in cars, computers, hospitals, buildings and more. Plastics are everywhere. However, as plastics have become so widespread, they have also become a huge pollution problem. Some plastics can take thousands of years to disintegrate and become absorbed into the environment. The problem has grown even larger in recent decades, causing concerns that some plastics containing toxic materials may cause a global health catastrophe.

the larger pieces of plastics in the ocean, not nearly enough people are even aware of microplastics. The more I thought about the problem of microplastics in the ocean, the more worried I felt.

Although I haven't yet seen a big chunk of plastic embedded in fish flesh, it's entirely possible that seafood includes microplastics we can't see. And that's bad, because plastics have been known to cause damage to an organism's lungs, heart and kidneys. Microplastics can even cause cancer or genetic mutations.

Plastics and other toxins slowly build up in the food chain

through two different processes. The first is bioaccumulation, where the level of toxins inside a single animal's body increases as the animal eats the plastics and can't get rid of them. The second is biomagnification, where toxins get more concentrated in each level of the food chain, as predators eat many other animals that have toxins inside their bodies.

Finally, the toxins reach the apex predators—which could be us. Eventually, plastics are likely to end up in all of our diets, no matter what we eat. It might be seafood, it might be livestock that consume seafood byproducts in their feed, or it even might be plants that use those livestock's manure as fertilizer. A recent study even shows that most of the salt brands that we use contain traces of microplastics. After I read that, even my favorite snack, salty pretzels, failed to cheer me up. Instead, every crunchy bite only led me to feel more anxious about this growing problem.

Just one afternoon of reading about plastics pollution had set my mind whirring. Worse, it was just my luck that the main part of dinner that evening was seafood. We were celebrating the arrival of my grandparents and my cousin, who had traveled to Massachusetts from Beijing for summer vacation. After learning that 73% of all fish have ingested plastics, and that plastic doesn't harmlessly pass through the animal's body—it often gets stuck in their bloodstream—I was a little reluctant to even touch the fish.

The only upside was that I could use my newfound information to torment my cousin. My cousin James is five years older than me, and our personalities clash. When we're together, we show our rivalry with daily arguments and pranks. Armed with my new information, I decided to needle him.

"Did you know that as plastics break down they sometimes bind with other potentially toxic materials to create an even more toxic hybrid? This can then spread into the food chain, which means that those toxic substances could be in that fish!" I said cheerfully.

James scoffed and rolled his eyes. Then he glanced warily at the steamed fish with shallots on his plate. He set down his fork.

"Anna!" my mom yelled.

"Sorry," I said, smirking.

Needless to say, James avoided seafood for a good time after.

What my parents hated the most was that the information I was spouting off was true.

Chapter 3

It's That Science Fair Time Of The Year Again

I sat down at my desk after I finished dinner, researching plastics again. This time, I focused more on cleanup efforts for plastics. After a bit of searching, I found many solutions online, and they all seemed to offer hopeful prospects. Some suggested large nets to corral ocean plastics onto the shore, and others proposed self-propelled vehicles to vacuum up the plastics.

Later that night, I was lying on the bed and thinking about that day's events...

"Wait a minute," I said to myself.

Something was missing. All the news reports and papers I had read so far only addressed how to eliminate large plastics.

The first and seemingly most popular method of cleaning plastics uses size-based filters. Some methods vacuumed ocean water through the nets. Some relied on natural forces like wind and currents to propel their nets and make the cleanup effort more efficient.

This method may work on larger pieces of plastics near the surface that are orders of magnitude larger than marine microorganisms. But microplastics can be tiny. They slip through the mesh. Even if someone made a net small enough to capture microplastics, many marine organisms would be caught up too. With no method of differentiating between plastics and plankton, removing all the microplastics from the ocean in this way would be deadly for the environment.

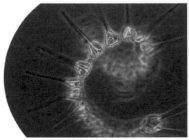

phytoplankton

Many labs have developed ways to identify plastics. One of the chemical-based methods that works the best is to use Nile Red Dye. Plastics dyed with Nile Red fluoresce under a filtered light of a specific blue wavelength. This method has proved accurate in identifying plastics. However, this method is also very invasive, as you need to dye the plastics themselves. Not to mention, methanol is used as a solvent for the dye. Methanol is extremely toxic to all animals, including humans. You can't dump bottle after bottle of methanol into the ocean, letting all the animals die as a result of your attempt to find plastics.

"But what about microplastics?" I exclaimed out loud.

None of the methods I had read about would work for microplastics. So what could be done? After a while of restless tossing and turning, I gave up trying to sleep.

Getting up from my bed, I turned on my desk light and took out

my notebook to brainstorm ideas. I tried my best to think deeply about what I had read earlier that day. Ocean vacuums and nets relied on size-based filters—which would trap large plastic chunks as they float by. But wouldn't they catch fish and turtles too? Not to mention, these tools would also miss all the tiny pieces.

Somehow, I had to break the problem down to a more fundamental level.

After writing that thought down, I was able to let go of my worrying long enough to fall asleep.

I was jarred awake when my dog licked my face, leaving a gooey trail of saliva that smelled a bit like salami.

"Eww, Andy!"

He licked me again, and my phone dinged. A friend was sending me a text.

"1 more month until school starts again. Can't wait for everything, especially science fair!"

Looking at that text made me want to groan. I couldn't honestly say I loved science fairs. In my school, starting in first grade, we're required to do science fair projects, even if we don't start competing until 6th grade. My projects were never very original. Not only were they extremely simple, but they were also mind-numbingly boring.

But as I set the phone down, I reflected that this problem with plastics was something I was really concerned about. What if I tried a science fair project on cleaning up microplastics in the ocean?

Before this, science had seemed so distant. After all, how could an 11-year-old come up with something new, something that mattered? When I read books or watched TV about science & engineering topics, it was easy to get the impression that everything in the world has already been invented. But what if I had a chance to make a potentially significant impact on the world? My teachers would give me time at school and at home, my parents would encourage me to work on my project. I might even be able to get out of some chores :)

In my sleepy early-morning state, I scribbled vague thoughts down on a scratch pad. I wanted to find and potentially get rid of plastics in the ocean. More specifically, microplastics. I only stopped scribbling when my dad called me to eat my morning fried rice.

I sat down at my desk right after my meal. I took out my notebook and jotted down some of the ideas floating around in my head. I remembered how light that first piece of plastic felt when I picked it up. Perhaps I could use density as a method to identify plastics. But after a little research, I quickly dismissed that idea. It turns out that different types of plastics have different densities— PVC, which is commonly used in plumbing, would sink in salt water, and PETE, which is used in everyday materials such as water bottles, would float. Even worse, microplastics change in

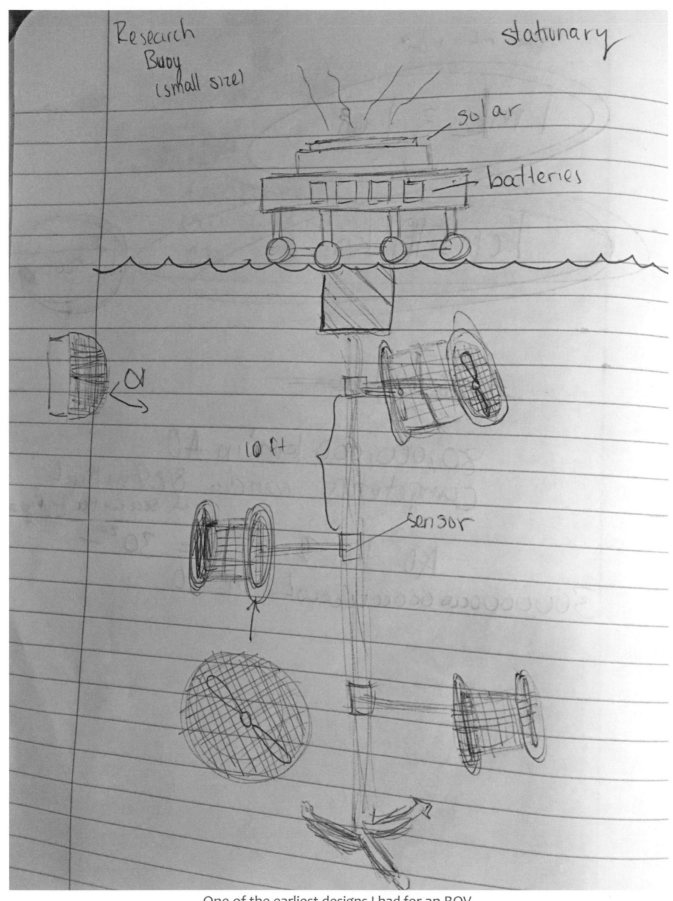

Research
Buoy
(small size)

stationary

solar

batteries

α

10 ft

sensor

One of the earliest designs I had for an ROV.
At this stage, I was focused on cleaning up the plastics more than locating them.

density as they break up and bind to other materials.

I needed to become more familiar with everyday plastics. Going into collector mode, I looked around the house for different objects that I could use for plastic samples. I found a list of what type of plastic made up what type of common household object, and I labeled my samples accordingly. I found:

- High-density polyethylene (HDPE): Plastic bags from our recent grocery trip

- Polypropylene (PP): Straws from a recent party

- Polyethylene terephthalate (PETE): Water bottles handed out at the gas station

- Polystyrene (PS): Foam peanuts from packaging

- Acrylonitrile butadiene styrene (ABS): Lego pieces from years ago, when James and I competed to build the best structures

- Polyester (PES): Even my clothes had plastics in them

Carrying my collection of samples with me, I ran to tell my parents, grandparents, and cousin about my idea. After all, they were the people always telling me to chase my dreams, try to make a difference, and care about the environment.

While I talked, my parents and grandparents smiled and nodded, commenting about how much I had learned already. My cousin smiled and nodded along with them, but then he spoke up with false concern. My eyes narrowed.

"Are you sure about this? I mean, you aren't exactly known for being the most motivated person in the family, and I will hate to see you disappointed when you finally give up," he said sweetly.

My parents considered what he was saying, making slight noises of assent.

"I suppose it's all about the learning experience," my dad said.

My mom added. "While James has a point, if you're able to prove to us that you're willing to spend your time wisely and you manage to keep on doing this while still keeping your grades up, we will be more than willing to help you. Just don't make a mess."

So that was that.

However, once my parents and grandparents left the room, my cousin's attitude hardened.

"You'll never carry this through," he told me.

I crossed my arms, saying, "I don't exactly see you doing something to help the environment."

"You're just like a butterfly, flitting around from one thing to another, getting all the attention. You can't focus on this for very long even if you try your best! Let's see how long this lasts."

"But... butterflies... they're important to the environment too! They're good... pollinators!" I spluttered.

He rolled his eyes and stalked away.

My cousin's behavior stung, so I steeled myself. It's true that I'm not the most disciplined person. Rather than sticking with one hobby, I do tend to flit around, losing interest quickly. However, this was something I could do if I put my mind to it. It was a problem I could solve. Along the way, I would prove to James I was more than just a butterfly.

ANNA'S
SCIENCE FAIR TIPS

MAKE SURE YOU WORK ON A TOPIC YOU CARE ABOUT. If you end up doing a multiphase project, your topic could be something that you end up working on for many years. Hopefully it's something you can not only stick with for a long time, as far as research agenda, but it's also something that makes you feel really interested and passionate!

Chapter 4

Elementary, My Dear Watson

Summer seemed to be passing quickly. I sat at the picnic table in the yard enjoying a slight breeze as I flipped through my notebook, which was now filled with notes on plastics and potential solutions.

I wanted to figure out the differences between plastics and microplastics. Besides size, I wondered if there were other differences. And why, despite the fact that many people already know a lot about microplastics, were so few people focused on microplastics as part of the cleanup problem?

Maybe it was because no one really knew exactly where in the ocean microplastics might be piling up. With the larger, more visible pieces of plastics on the surface of the ocean, it's different. Travel to the right place and you can see the plastics right there on the surface. Scientists can even predict where these surface plastics will gather. They can follow the flow of the gyres, which are global patterns of ocean currents caused by wind, waves, and the Coriolis effect. These gyres cause the plastics to group together in garbage patches. In fact, if you take a look at a detailed world ocean current map, you can find all of the garbage patches by simply finding the centers of the gyres.

Suddenly, Andy started barking crazily and put his paws on the fence. I knew immediately that the mailman had come. This is a case where Andy acts more like a protector than a younger brother. On the other hand, if you come to my house with a hamburger in your hands, he would be happy to be your brother too.

Hearing Andy bark, the mailman hesitated in his car. All at once he opened the door, ran out, and almost threw the package down. Then he sprinted back to the car, shut the door, and drove away fast. I always find it funny how people can fear Andy when he's more like a giant teddy bear than anything else.

I picked up the package, ripped open the cardboard box and took out all of the bubble wrap... only to find another box inside. There was so much plastic packaging! I wondered what my mother had bought me.

I opened up the box, and inside, I found a chemistry model set! In it were toy atoms you could use to model the shape of a molecule. I remembered a lesson on photosynthesis from last year's science class. We learned that plants photosynthesize and turn sunlight, carbon dioxide, and water into glucose and oxygen. Glucose—that was the monomer for starch. My mom was giving me a hint. I could use this chemistry set to make models of plastic polymers.

The Periodic Table of the Elements

	alkali metals		metalloids
	alkaline metals		nonmetals
	other metals		halogens
	transition metals		noble gases
	lanthanoids		unknown elements
	actinoids	☢	radioactive elements have masses in parenthesis

Many plastic have the same elements as the basic organic chemicals of living things (CHON).

I knew that the formula for glucose was $C_6H_{12}O_6$—six carbons, twelve hydrogens, and six oxygens. Working at the picnic table, I started snapping red, blue, and white "atoms" together. However, I just couldn't seem to get all the elements to fit. So I fetched my laptop and searched for glucose. It turned out that the shape of my molecule really mattered! After I finally built my first glucose molecule, a flexible hexagon, I grinned widely. It felt like a Matrix moment, where the whole world suddenly became a bunch of spinning bits and bytes—only for me it was atoms and molecules. It occurred to me that everything around me was made up of different combinations of elements.

A glucose model

Now, my curiosity had been piqued, and I Googled other polymers, especially the six types of plastics I had collected earlier. I wanted to see how their molecular structures differed from one another. When I was searching them up, I found the structure for nylon, and I built it immediately. When I had made them all, I put my model molecules in front of each sample I had collected. I tried to figure out how their molecular structure influenced their look, texture, stiffness, flexibility, and elasticity.

Just looking at the different types of molecule models themselves, especially glucose, I could see that their structures were very different. For instance, nylon, which is found in clothing, had a long and open structure that appeared elastic. It was clearly more flexible than glucose, which is stiffer and harder. I felt l had achieved a personal breakthrough. Despite the fact that all these molecules were made using the same basic elements, the differences in the way they were bonded led to different characteristics.

I learned that plastics, being man-made polymers, have similar chemical compounds to those found in living things. They're all organic (carbon-containing) compounds with the same basic elements, such as carbon, nitrogen, oxygen, and hydrogen. Differences in how they bond are too small to detect easily but big enough to wreak havoc on the environment. The bonds within plastics are stronger than those in natural compounds, making them harder to break down. But the fact that plastics are so similar in structure to natural compounds makes it hard to identify plastics and separate them from marine animals without harming the environment.

Chapter 5

A New Mentor

School started, and I learned from one of my teachers that there was going to be a lecture about careers and science fairs at a local university. I asked my dad to drive me. To my surprise, the speaker turned out to be a polymer guru named Dr. Jon. He's a senior researcher at a major local company that makes polymers for the semiconductor, automobile, and other high-tech industries. His speech inspired me.

After some hesitation, I wrote Dr. Jon an email to see if he might be willing to mentor a twelve-year-old girl like me. As soon as I hit "send" I thought to myself, *Well that was probably a waste of time. He'll never respond.*

Minutes later I heard a ding from my computer. I was amazed to see that he had responded almost immediately!

Hello Anna,

I grew up with my dad as a scientist and it was sometimes challenging even then. You have a very good project idea.

Dr. Jon Siddall, of Cabot, lectures at MIT's MA State Science Fair

I am happy to help you. Polymer analysis is less precise than analysis of small molecules. Mixtures of polymers are especially challenging. You would expect some polymers to bind heavy metals, but many probably would be inert.

Let's talk about this on the phone and see what we can do. A call after school hours is ok almost every day this week. Please let me know a day and time that are best for you. If possible, I'd like to include one of our analysis experts.

Jon

A few days later, I sat in my room, my hands shaking. I sucked in a deep breath and pressed the 'pick-up' button. This was my first time on the phone with a scientist as famous as he was. In fact, it was really the first time

I'd spoken with any adult other than close family members or teachers for any real length of time. In my nervousness I must have repeated the same things over and over again. He was surprisingly patient and kind to me. After the phone call, I wrote back right away.

Dear Dr. Jon,

Thank you so much for calling me. I'm sorry I was a bit nervous today, I have never really had the chance to talk to such a knowledgeable scientist like yourself before.

I found the advice you gave me very informative, especially on the idea that polymers being long chains are less reactive when they're longer chains (in the center of the block of material as opposed to edges), and when they've broken apart due to brittleness, the ends become more reactive. This is a very fascinating way of describing chemically what is going on with the microplastic density changes.

Thank you for all the help you have given me so far.

Sincerely,

Anna

The next day, I waited anxiously for his email reply. I wasn't sure how he would respond—did I speak too immaturely? Would he think that I didn't know my subject as well as he thought? When I got home from school, I lunged for my computer. His response stared at me from the Unread Emails section.

Hi, Anna,

Regarding your idea, I make a few comments.

A central part of your hypothesis is that the plastic density changes when it is out in the environment. The tests we have been talking about above do not directly address this. Many small life forms do not have any mineral content, so they probably are about the same density as water. Heavy metals are only a few parts per million, so even if they built up hundreds of times that on the plastic they would only change the density a tiny amount. Now if something slimy grows on the particles, then the slime might catch sand or shelled sea life like diatoms and make them sink pretty well.

HDPE has a density of about 0.97 g/cc, while sea water is 1.02 to 1.03, so all polyethylenes will float in the ocean. PVC is a whopping 1.38, so it sinks like a rock, even in the Dead Sea, which is 1.24.

Have you had algebra yet? If so, here is a fun calculation:

Problem statement: As it floats in the ocean, a one gram sample of HDPE starts to become covered in diatoms (density 2.0) How many grams of diatoms must the piece of plastic accumulate until the density of the piece reaches that of seawater, 1.03 g/cc?

We can speak again—the main thing is to figure out exactly what we will test and find a way to make it happen in time.

Jon

These were just the first of many emails that we sent each other. Over time, Dr. Jon taught me many essential things. It turns out that nowadays, people are not only studying how plastics are made, but also how they break down. In fact, Dr. Jon told me that time and light affect how polymers break down. Instead of being flexible and rubbery, plastics that are exposed to time and light become denser and more brittle. The material properties themselves are changed. Then, as plastics break down, the ends of broken molecules become more reactive, allowing for more chemical reactions and binding with other materials.

ANNA'S SCIENCE FAIR TIPS

THINK GLOBAL. When picking a science fair topic, you should try your best to choose a project that helps solve a world problem or helps others in some way. In some cases, if your interests are in theoretical areas of science or engineering, it may be difficult to make a claim that you're solving a world problem. However, regardless of what your primary topic is, it's always a good thing to describe alternate applications of your work, in other related fields as well.

Chapter 6

A Sea Of Microplastics

A few days later, in school, my class was learning about surface area. As our teacher explained the formula for calculating the surface area of a cylinder, it hit me. If you sliced a cylinder in two, all at once you'd have two more cylinder ends than before. As plastics break into separate pieces, their surface area must increase also. This would mean that the areas where plastics could potentially bind with other materials would slowly increase over time. I was excited to discuss this with Dr. Jon, and I ran to my room as soon as I got home.

"Boo!" It was James. He had been hiding behind my door to prank me.

"James, you jerk, get out of my room," I yelled.

"What are you working on, butterfly—let me see," he said, grabbing for my laptop.

"Who's this guy writing to you? Is he your boyfriend?" James asked, trying to be as annoying as he possibly could.

"Oh my god. Seriously? He's a scientist who's helping me with my project. I'm writing to him about surface area. Now why are you still here? Get out, now!" I exclaimed.

"Surface area? Are you kidding me? I learned that years ago, maybe even in kindergarten. In my school we're way ahead of you guys in math. Don't you know that? I bet you don't know anything about geometry at all. I know a trick I bet you don't know. How many times do you think you can break a brand-new pencil in half?"

"I dunno, I guess I break pencils all the time. Probably like 4 or 5. Why?" I said.

"Ok, let's try it. I think you can't do it more than twice."

I pulled out a new pencil and went for it. Once, twice, Snap! —no problem. But then the third time, I genuinely had a hard time.

"OK, you're right," I said, as I shoved James out of my room. I didn't want to hear his explanation. If he helped out with my project in any way, I'd never hear the end of it for the rest of my life. So I decided to look it up myself.

After doing a bit of research, I decided that James was somewhat right. This was a pretty relevant and interesting exercise. It turns out that geometry has a lot to do with how and why materials can break down. I could feel instinctively that this was going to somehow be useful knowledge for my project, but what did it all really mean?

Maybe it meant that plastics would become more and more

stable over time. Like the grains of sand on a beach, as time goes by, chemicals and physical forces cause rocks to break down, and they become more and more stable shapes. I'd have to think more about it.

Later that evening I replied to Jon's most recent email:

Dear Dr. Jon,

I actually have tried to do some fun experiments involving plastic densities before, at programs [at MIT]. I've attached some pics. Basically, you can end up with plastics perfectly neutrally buoyant or plastics separated on the top and bottom of concentrated salt solutions in alcohol. One of my first thoughts regarding how to remove microplastics from the ocean was that density could be used somehow. But it seems that so many toxic chemicals or high pressures need to be used and that

Microplastics: An issue of Surface Area

While plastic pollution has become a huge global problem, and has been known for many decades, the issue of microplastics is a relatively recent one. And, it's not necessarily because microplastics are more toxic. In fact, these small particles are made up of the same chemicals as the larger ones that you can find on nearly every beach in the world. It's also not necessarily due to how widespread larger plastic trash is vs microplastic trash in the ocean and on land. They are both pretty widespread forms of pollution all around the Earth. In fact, the issue is really about relatively simply geometry. As plastics break down, due to sunlight UV, wave action, and other forces in the ocean, they expose new, fresh surface areas along the edges, where the particles break. These "new" edges serves as very active areas for biologicals, organic chemicals and even toxic materials to attach. As these pieces break down further and further, they have increasing amounts of surface area. As a single piece of plastic breaks down further and further into smaller microplastics, this causes a potential exponential increase in the surface area that plastics attach to, thus becoming potentially more toxic—and more widespread than ever before. And this problem is only getting larger over time.

Looking at the following formula, you can see the increase in surface area vs volume of material as follows:

As the table below shows, if you break a 3 m cubed cube into 27 1 m cubed pieces , you increase the surface area from 54 m² to 27 x 6 m², which is 162 m².

would cause so much sea life to die, that it would defeat the purpose.

Yes, I did take Algebra, and I do some math for fun at home most nights. I'm pretty sure that the answer to your question is roughly 0.13g. I got it by M_HDPE * (d / d_ HDPE - 1) / (1 - d / d_ diatom). Believe it or not, I actually really enjoy doing math :)

Hope to hear from you soon again. Thanks again so much. I am writing this right before bed, so I'm a bit sleepy now.

Total surface area (height x width x sides x numbers of boxes)	6m²	24m²	54m²
Total volume (height x width x length x numbers of boxes)	1m³	8m³	27m³
SA: Vol ratio (Surface area to volume ratio)	6:1	3:1	2:1

Hope you have a nice day.

Sincerely,

Anna

I did more research every time I emailed Dr. Jon. I found out that microplastics get into the ocean through multiple pathways. Some enter the ocean already as microplastics, such as from your mom's cosmetics, or from your toothpaste. (Bet you didn't know those had microplastics in them.) The others, which start off as larger pieces of plastics, all have different stories. These particles might be broken down through biological processes. For example, sea turtles swallow plastic bags, thinking they're jellyfish, and fish eat plastics too, such as broken-up water bottles or bottle caps, then poop them out.

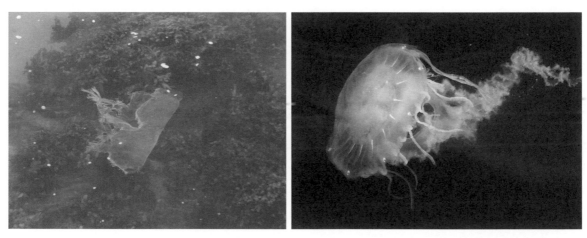

Plastic bag floating in a marine harbour (left) has a close resemblance to jellyfish (right).

Plastics can also be broken down by physical forces such as the constant motion of the waves. Or they can be broken down by chemical processes, for example when they're damaged by ultraviolet light. Their chemical structures break down, and eventually they divide into smaller and smaller pieces. As time passes by, plastics gradually gain density, mostly by bonding to heavier compounds. Finally they sink to the ocean floor. Though the life experiences of these plastics are different, their fates are the same.

Once plastics reach the bottom of the ocean, things get way more interesting. On the surface, conditions are somewhat predictable. But on the bottom of the ocean, it's a completely different world—there is no wind, and surface waves don't affect currents that are so deep. So what does happen down there? We know water movements could be affected by temperature, salinity, density, topology (terrain) and other factors. Maybe it's all so complicated that microplastics' final destiny is unpredictable after all. They're all going to get lost in the ocean. Not to mention, as microplastics circulate over and over again through the life cycles of countless animals in the marine ecosystem, these particles seem destined to spread farther and farther. All at once, my dreams of making a difference seemed quite hopeless.

That night as I prepared to go to sleep, it occurred to me that maybe James was right—maybe I didn't have the math skills and engineering knowledge needed to solve such a huge problem. Maybe it was time for this butterfly to flutter on to something else. Something... simpler.

Chapter 7

Maybe This Will Work

Friday after school meant another trip to the beach. Beach trips always offer a good way for me and Andy to have some wet and salty fun. This time, I prepared two bags. One bag was for sea glass and the second bag for plastic trash. Even if I wasn't sure about my science fair project, I still knew that I wanted to pick up the trash.

As I walked along the beach, Andy followed me. A life-long lover of sticks, he kept bringing me his favorite toy. As I bent down to pick up a particularly bright piece of plastic, I looked back for him and realized that he kept returning to the same area, thirty feet from the shore. That was where he found all his sticks. I then noticed that I was sticking around one area too, maybe ten feet from the shore, along a band filled with shells and sea glass. Looking toward the water, I noticed that all of the heavy rocks were in one band as well—right next to the shore. Even the sand itself seemed to display a sort of gradient of textures along the coastline. I realized that the beach was sorting itself in different ways. I found myself thinking about my project almost against my will.

This led me to a new thought. If these seemingly random materials were being sorted, why shouldn't the same kind of sorting happen with microplastics at the bottom of the ocean? When we learned about density in school, our teacher mentioned that in a river with gold deposits, the gold always ends up in the bends of the river. This is because gold suspended in water moves best in regions with high water flow. The intense movement and mixing of water is called turbidity. However, when there is less turbidity, in corners and bends— places where rivers slow down—the gold sinks. That is why all the gold ends up aggregating in one place. That's what made it possible for California miners in the 1800s to "pan" for gold.

The Great Pacific Garbage Patch is really no different from this. The regions where ocean current flow is lowest—in the center of gyres—is where all the large plastics end up. So, since nature has this ever-present tendency to sort things according to size and density, that must mean that there are probably large "microplastic patches" on the ocean floor.

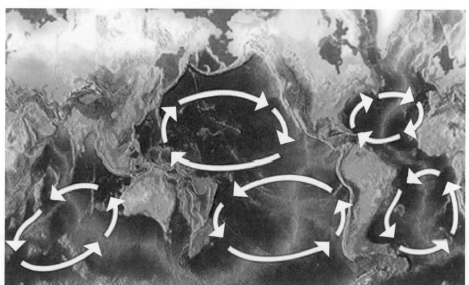

Gyres & The Great Pacific Garbage Patch

Gyres are giant, permanent, swirling currents, somewhat like whirlpools, that can be found throughout our oceans. These currents are due to the Coriolis effect of the Earth, or the spinning of the planet on its axis. Currently, there are 5 major gyres that have been identified, including one in the middle of the Pacific Ocean. The Great Pacific Garbage Patch, well off the coast of California, attracts lots of media attention due to its sheer size. By some estimates, this floating island of plastic is bigger than the state of Texas. That means that there are millions of floating plastic bottles, toys, widgets, grocery bags and more, that have the potential to be consumed by marine animals.

What concerns me even more is the potential that each floating bottle of water could one day break apart into thousands of microplastics, and spread further and further throughout the world's oceans and ultimately, our entire global food chain. Maybe the cumulative effect of so many pieces of plastic could mean that one day, researchers might just find a "Great Underwater Microplastic Patch."

After all, in order to make something related to nature, we need to learn about nature first. If we observe nature, we could learn a lot: the solution might be already there. I like to read about innovations inspired by nature. For example, Olympic athletes use swimwear that imitates the skins of dolphins and sharks, and Velcro is modeled after burdock burrs. Maybe, I thought, different types of microplastics gather in specific places. If we could study the various physical, chemical and other factors associated with deposits of plastics, such as pH, temperature, or salinity, maybe we could learn to predict where lots of microplastics might be found.

After all... wouldn't it be easier to find the problem first, before cleaning it up?

It would be sort of like Andy searching for sticks at the beach. Instead of looking through the entire beach, he knows that if he goes to that band a certain distance from the water, then he'll find a lot of sticks. Maybe there are areas like that underwater—areas that are sort of like plastic mines, hiding tons of microplastics.

This reminded me of a concept I recently read about in a book. A woman in the 1800's named Hertha Ayrton, against all odds, became a mathematician and physicist recognized by the Royal Society in England for her work on waves. During those days women weren't even allowed to have college degrees, and they were usually discouraged from academics. Despite that, Hertha became the first women to present her ideas in front of the Institution of Electrical Engineers; it's surprising to me that not too many people know about her.

One of Hertha Ayrton's biggest contributions to science was demonstrating that the waves you find in the patterns of electricity or even light are not much different from the waves in the ocean. This is the reason why electromagnetic waves (like infrared light waves) look like ocean waves when they represent them in diagrams. Hertha described how you can find these same wave patterns in ripples in the sand at low tide. Places where the sand deposits are areas where the velocity of the water is a little bit less than in other areas. I have a hunch that this same type of action might be happening to plastics underwater as well. They probably sort themselves into waves or pockets of particles and then mix with mud and sand and other particles, based somewhat on density. There are always patterns in the universe caused by the forces all around us.

So instead of trying to come up with ways to clean plastics up passively... maybe I should come up with a more active way to locate them first.

Ripple waves in the sand

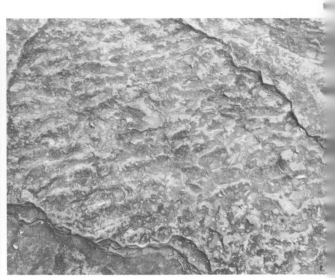

Fossilized ripple waves

ANNA'S
SCIENCE FAIR TIPS

RESEARCHING YOUR TOPIC IS ONE OF THE MOST IMPORTANT PROCESSES IN YOUR PROJECT. It creates the foundation, and gives you something to build upon. Not only do you need to research about the topic itself, you also should research about similar projects as well— though you don't want to copy what they did, it might help you come up with ideas, if you see what other people have done. You need to be absolutely sure that your idea is innovative.

Chapter 8

It's Finally Make Day!

The next day, hunger woke me up. I smelled fried rice and realized that my mom and dad were cooking breakfast down the hall. That meant it must be a Saturday! Or as I like to call it, "Make Day."

For years I've been attending an afternoon open makerspace workshop at MIT on weekends. It's probably my most creative time of the week. The workshop is a great outlet for me to have a little fun while picking up engineering skills. It seems to me that year by year, more maker places are popping up—at libraries, schools and even some maker cafes. At MIT's Saturday program, anyone can go in and build whatever they like with help from the experts there.

Fooling around in the makerspace is what made me realize I wanted to become an engineer. Every time I go, there's always some new challenge, whether it's making a machine that uses LEDs and a piece of glass to recreate what an aurora looks like, a density bottle, or a circuit. The possibilities are endless. This was where I went to when I wanted to create new things, or when I wanted to get expert advice.

The MIT makerspace was the place where I first learned how to build an ROV—a remotely operated underwater vehicle. I learned how to fix a sturdy shaft onto a motor, how to cut PVC, and how to design shapes for different purposes.

The person who mainly runs these programs is called Ed. He's sort of a mix between Indiana Jones, a very skinny Santa Claus, and Macgyver. He's always moving around, fixing things and building stuff, or helping students with their inventions. He has a talent for using ordinary materials to create simple solutions for all kinds of problems. This seemingly magical skill has earned him the awe of all the students and the respect of the faculty at MIT.

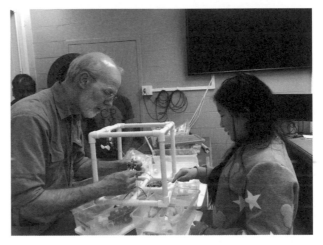

Ed and me

One of my first impressions of him came from hearing him one day heartily belt out the theme song to Mister Ed, a TV show from the 1960s.

Ooooooooooooh,
A horse is a horse, of course, of course,
And no one can talk to a horse, of course,
Unless, of course, the horse, of course,

Is the famous Mister Ed!

That's why he is affectionately known to his inner circle as "Mr. Ed."

One particular Saturday, Mr. Ed asked us to do a basic engineering challenge. He asked us to build a structure with the smallest possible base and the widest top, using the fewest possible parts. Ed told us that in the end, he would show us a surprise structure that he was sure would beat everyone else's.

Sediment Experiment at MIT Edgerton Center

In the end, we kids in the workshop built many different types of structures, usually using dozens of pieces. There were ones shaped like a cross with the top cut off, and there were ones shaped like a bowl. Out of all the competitors, one group seemed to be in the lead with a structure that seemed to look like a big bowl with only edges and no sides.

Until Ed brought out his structure. It was extremely simple, just a single piece that had all the key requirements of the challenge. I won't give away his secret here— but needless to say, we were all surprised by its simplicity. He had even purposefully walked around while we were building, asking if anyone wanted to use the piece. In the end, his solution worked better than any others.

The point that Ed was trying to make was that in engineering, if you make a simpler design, there are fewer potential points of failure, and that's more likely to be the best solution. At MIT, we're constantly reminded of Occam's razor, which essentially means that the best solution is the simplest.

I learned a very valuable engineering lesson: always keep it simple.

After the challenge, I went up to Ed and his colleague David, who is an MIT alumnus and volunteer mentor for the maker lab. David worked as an engineer for Mitsubishi for over thirty years. I asked them for advice on my project. I wanted to know how I could design an underwater vehicle that could aid me in my quest to find and clean up microplastics.

"What would be a great way for me to design a really maneuverable underwater vehicle, or something like that?" I asked.

"You could research some famous ROVs out there," David suggested. "Do you know Jason?"

"Umm... I don't think I've ever met him, no."

Ed and David laughed.

"No, no, no, we're not talking about a him, we're talking about an it," David explained. "Jason is the first ROV to ever have a scientific mission, created by Woods Hole Oceanographic Institution. Search it up!"

At the lab, we're encouraged to learn things by ourselves and explore for our own curiosity, instead of the normal way, behind a desk with a teacher lecturing at the front. Ed and

Talking to David about Jason

David never give us a direct answer, preferring to tell us to learn by ourselves.

"Another example is Nereid," Ed added. "Do a bit of research on that too."

When I searched it up, I realized that Jason was created to find the Titanic. The Nereid, however, was the vessel I found even more interesting. It was the first low-cost way of exploring the life under the ice in the Arctic. I noticed that these two ROVs are similar in one way—both are shaped like cubes. Weird. I went back to Ed.

"I thought the shapes of underwater vehicles were inspired by marine animals. I've heard that the latest ones are even modeled after tuna, to gain more speed. So, why are these vehicles basically just boxes? It seems sort of clunky and counter-intuitive to me."

Top: ROV Jason. Middle and bottom: The Nereid, a Hybrid Remotely Operated Vehicle (HROV), built by Woods Hole Oceanographic Institution, capable of operating at extreme depths (~11,000m!)

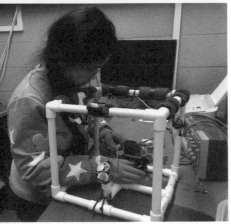

Using the engineering design process to build my first ROV

Ed said, "Good observation! What you're saying is true. For ROVs that are shaped like an animal, the main objective is speed. However, for Jason and the Nereid, the main objective is not speed. Rather, they're both trying to observe something. In these two ROVs, accuracy is more important than the speed. That's why they aren't shaped like an animal."

"Huh, that's cool! I think I'm going to name my ROV the Nereid Jr.," I said with a smile on my face.

This was another valuable engineering lesson I learned that day—sometimes, accuracy is more important than speed.

At MIT Edgerton Center

Chapter 9

The Sort Game

" Anna, come here!" my mom yelled.

I sighed and got to my feet. My mom held out her phone, and I was greeted with the images of my aunt, uncle, and James waving. Now that school was in full swing, they were back in Beijing. To me, James's wave looked much less enthusiastic than his parents'.

"I'll leave you two cousins to talk to each other," my aunt said, sending James a meaningful glance.

It was amazing how we seemed to roll our eyes in unison. Once everyone left for a different room, James turned up the sarcasm.

"So, Butterfly, how's your plastics project? My mom said that you've already told your school this is going to be your science fair topic. Puh-lease. You're way over your head."

I bristled at "Butterfly." My parents and grandparents all thought it was some new affectionate nickname from one loving cousin to another.

"I bet I know more than you about plastics, big shot!" I retorted.

"Oh yeah? Do you want to test that?"

"Why not," I said, my glare hardening.

His eyes narrowed.

I pressed on. "If you're able to tell me the correct name of five different types of plastic, and one daily appliance each one could be used for, and I can't, then I'll agree with you. Maybe I'm not qualified to do this project. However, if you can't do it and I can, then you have to stop pestering me about this project. Capeesh?"

"Capeesh."

I smiled sweetly at James. He seemed to regret this whole bet now, but I knew his pride would never allow him to actually quit.

"Ready?" I asked, trying to school my facial expression into innocence.

He rolled his eyes in a last attempt to regain his dignity and nodded stiffly.

"3... 2... 1... go!"

Demonstrating the best way to sort and separate trash for recycling

"Uh... PVC... is used with... microwaves? Um... no, no... it's used in... plumbing and... um... Polyester... is in telephones... yeah um..." he trailed off.

I waited a moment to see if he would respond, but he remained silent, so I started talking.

"Uh huh. Nice try. PVC is used in plumbing, but not in microwaves. I don't even know where you got that idea. Polyester is used in clothing. Who told you that it was put in telephones?

"What else. Let's see... acrylic is used in paint, polyethylene terephthalate is used in water bottles, polyurethane is used in construction to waterproof materials such as ships, polyvinyl alcohol is used in detergent, and polystyrene is used in eating utensils," I finished smugly.

He huffed, then turned around, ignoring me.

"Well, I thought this was a fun game," I said.

James hung up. Then footsteps thundered behind me, followed by the thud of a gigantic black trash bag by my side. As I turned around, I saw that my mom's face was completely red. She folded her arms in front of her.

"Anna, what is this mess in your room? How long has that food been sitting out on your desk? It must have been there for days. Has it? Not to mention there's junk all over the house. Did you forget your chores? TAKE OUT THE TRASH NOW!" Her hands waved in the air. "Go now!"

I considered telling her I'd take out the trash later, but when she talks like that, she really means business. I chose silent obedience. As my mom stormed off into the other room, still mumbling complaints to herself. I ran around the house grabbing all the bags from the trash bins in the bathrooms. When I ran into the kitchen, what I saw before me shocked me. No wonder my mom was so mad. Trash bags lay in piles next to the fridge, left over from a party my parents had held the day before.

"Oh, man," I said out loud, as I realized what a huge pile of trash I'd need to lug out to the garage.

As I went to grab the largest bag, my mom yelled, "Are you done yet?"

Startled, I dropped the bag, and trash spilled everywhere—water bottles rolled under the counter, paper plates, plastic forks and spoons that seemed almost unused scattered under the table. It was like our own Great Pacific Garbage Patch right in the kitchen. I couldn't believe how much plastic trash one small group of people could throw out after a single neighborhood party.

"Are you kidding me?" my mom asked from the doorway as she stared in disbelief at the mess before her.

"Sorry," I said, "I...um."

"I don't want to hear it," my mom said. "Just clean it up quickly and get all these bags outside. Now you also have to wipe up the floor when you get back too. Do it. Right now!" She stood over me, fuming. I nearly expected to see smoke coming out of her ears.

I picked up another trash bag and started to put fork after knife after spoon into it, as quickly as I could. Suddenly a thought hit me. I paused for a moment, wondering whether it would be a good idea for me to talk to my mom in her present state, but I just couldn't help myself. I held up a shiny new plastic fork.

"Mom, look at all these plastic utensils—they don't even look used. Why dump all this plastic into the trash? Why don't we recycle these or just wash them and reuse them?"

My mom looked close to exploding.

"Just clean it up!"

I stared at all the plastics around the kitchen floor. Shaking my head, I started sorting them. The plastics and other recyclables went in one pile and the non-recyclables in another. However, just sorting the contents of one trash bag was taking me a long time, and halfway through, I was already feeling antsy to do something else.

Andy padded into the room and started to sniff around, messing up the piles I'd already made. He licked one of the dirtier plates.

"Eww, Andy, go away!" I said, pushing him out of the room. He gave me a look that clearly asked, *What did I do?*

I breathed in, shook my head, and started sorting again. This was just one bag, for one, small, neighborhood party. There are tens of thousands of people in my town, and there are a couple of hundred towns and cities in my state. If this was how much plastic one party generated, and there were so many people in my state alone, who could be hosting many of these parties every single day... I wondered how recycling companies could sort plastics on such a large scale.

Chapter 10

How Do Recycling Companies Do It?

Even after I finished sorting and lugged out the trash and recycling, I couldn't get that question out of my mind. I begged my parents to take me to the town hall to find out what companies ran recycling companies in our area.

At the town hall, the lady behind the desk took an interest in my project.

"Oh, that's very interesting! I think it's so important that people are growing more and more concerned about the environment, and that young people are trying to learn more!"

She handed me papers and smiled. "Here's some information. Kids like you give me hope for the future."

After we left, my mom leafed through the pieces of paper. She started tutting.

"Look at this! There are signs everywhere encouraging us to recycle, yet they hardly let us recycle anything," she said, passing sheets of paper to me.

To my dismay, I saw that she was right. We weren't allowed to recycle plastic bags, straws, styrofoam, food containers, coat hangers, plastic eating utensils, or most objects we use every day. We were barely allowed to recycle anything!

"Why do they do that?" I asked.

My mom shook her head. "I guess you'll have to find out when you visit the recycling company."

A few days later, my parents brought me to the first company on the list. When I got there, I met a young man wearing a Red Sox baseball hat. He patiently listened as I gave him a quick description of my project, and he even gave me a tour of the facility. While we walked, I asked questions.

"How do you sort all of these pieces of plastics and other recyclables that come in? A few days ago, I was trying to clean up just one garbage bag's worth of plastic, and that took me a long time. I can't imagine sorting this entire town's recycling!"

Infrared (IR) Spectroscopy

Infrared is the type of light that powers our TV remote controls, and is the same type of light that is used by police SWAT teams and the military to look through buildings to locate people. It's also used at fast food restaurants to keep food warm. Just outside the visible spectrum (on the red side of the spectrum rainbow), infrared has many other lesser-known uses. Aside from its uses in modern engineering, infrared is also an important part of our natural world, as well. It is a major reason why the greenhouse effect works, causing climate change. However, it also has a very practical use in the world of chemistry as an analytical tool. Many materials absorb and reflect infrared light very differently, and in specific patterns, which can be used to differentiate between specific types of organic compounds. This is due to the fact that "near" infrared is particularly

"It's pretty difficult. We'd like to recycle plastics, but there are very few commercially buyable pieces of plastic. To simply put it, it costs more money to recycle most plastic items than to make new ones. There's not much market. I mean, there is this new thing called Precious Plastics—but it's just the beginning of an idea at this point. And sometimes, when a piece of plastic has been recycled too many times, it can't be recycled again."

I frowned. "So how do you clean up pieces of plastic?"

"We first use density to sort through all the materials, and to get a main idea of which of these materials are plastics and which aren't. Then we use infrared spectroscopy to differentiate among the different types of plastics. Once they're sorted, we wash them to get rid of non-plastic residues such as stickers, leftover food, that kind of thing. These non-plastics would cause poor structural integrity if they weren't cleaned off."

"What happens once the plastics are cleaned?"

"We shred them, and then use a metal detector along with magnets to get rid of any leftover metal. Then, we melt the pieces and make them into small pellets, which can then be used to manufacture new products, such as the fleece sweatshirt you're wearing today, plastic water bottles, or even those squishies you kids seem to like these days."

"That's so cool!" I told him. "I made a metal detector once, to try to find gold on a beach. But do you think I could use a spectrometer in my project to differentiate plastics from non-plastics?"

The young man only chuckled, saying, "That depends how rich you are. How much gold did you find? A spectrometer costs tens of thousands of dollars!"

great at detecting certain organic chemical bonds in molecules. For instance, infrared light can be used to clearly tell the difference between sugars and plastics, and even different types of plastics. That makes it very useful to chemists, as well as recycling companies. Infrared spectroscopy, which is a technology I use in my project, uses very carefully measured infrared light to construct absorption graphs of different materials, in order to study and compare them. This technology can also be used to visualize different materials as well, making it easy to "see" plastics among other materials.

I gasped. "Tens of thousands?"

"Or more," he said with a careless shrug. "Infrared spectrometers aren't cheap."

I bit my lip. "Isn't there a cheaper way? I mean, I really only need this to be able to identify the difference between plastics and non-plastics, like sand, I don't need it to be so specific that it can differentiate between, say, polyester and polyethylene."

He shrugged again. "Could be. I don't see how you can make money out of that, but I'm sure it's possible."

"I'm not really doing this for the money," I told him in a virtuous tone. "My goal is to save marine life." Until that moment, making money off my project hadn't crossed my mind.

He laughed. "Maybe not all marine life is that valuable—I've been watching Shark Week lately."

We clearly weren't on the same wavelength. I finished scribbling down his words, thanked him, and left.

Chapter 11

Een – frah – red?

I couldn't wait to go to the maker lab again and show Mr. Ed some of my designs. I had lots of questions I wanted to ask him, especially about spectroscopy.

My favorite thing about Ed is that he never directly answers your question, and you end up learning a lot more than if you had just received your answer. Once I asked him about current and voltage. He spent the entire morning talking about water flow and Japanese water fountains. At the end of that class, I learned not only a lot about currents and voltage, but also about DC and AC, transistors and capacitors.

"So, do you know how infrared spectroscopy works?" I asked, holding my plastic samples, as soon as I saw that he was done working with the other students.

"Before I answer any questions, tell me what you've been working on," he said.

"Well, I want to create a machine that can identify plastics in the ocean. A couple days ago, I went to a recycling company to see how they identify and sort plastics, and it turns out that they use infrared spectroscopy. But the man said a spectroscope is very expensive. I'm wondering if there's a cheaper way."

"Mmm hmm. Do you know the electromagnetic spectrum?"

"Umm... I've heard of it before," I replied.

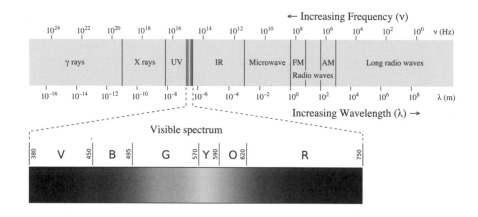

electromagnetic spectrum

"Okay. I have an idea for an experiment we can do. We're going to take the temperature of light!"

I followed him. Experiments with Mr. Ed were always informative and fun. He brought me into the storage room and asked me to find three thermometers and a piece of white paper.

I rifled through the drawers section. Everything was labeled alphabetically.

Batteries... LEDs... resistors... There! Thermometers. I grabbed a sheet of paper from a stack and brought both materials to him. He was already holding a small cardboard box and a glass prism.

We assembled the device together, with him telling me where all the pieces should go. Then he brought it to an open window. We positioned the box so the sun shone on the prism, casting a rainbow on the white paper. We arranged the three thermometers: the first one in the blue region, the second one in the yellow, and the third just past the red.

After we waited a minute, I noticed something.

"Wait... Why is the thermometer that isn't even on the rainbow warmer than the actual rainbow?"

"You've just discovered the infrared part of the electromagnetic spectrum," he told me. "This rainbow contains the lights you can see. To the left and to the right of the rainbow, though you can't see them, are other lights, including infrared and ultraviolet. This entire thing is called the electromagnetic spectrum."

"So they're sort of like invisible waves."

"Exactly!" Ed nodded. "We all know light, it travels with a constant speed, always the same. Different waves have different wavelengths. The smaller the wavelength, the higher the waves' frequencies are, and the more energy they carry. Gamma rays are really short waves with really high energy, and they can be used to treat cancer. X-rays can see through your body. UV lights can kill bacteria. Microwaves, which are long waves, can be used to heat up your food. Radio waves work for your cell phones and radios."

My brows furrowed in confusion. "But when we were doing the experiment, wasn't the infrared section hotter than the section with visible light? How would the visible light have more energy than infrared?"

I am using bread board circuit testing infrared LED with different wavelengths.

Ed laughed. "That experiment that we just did was primarily concerned with proving the fact that there were other parts of the electromagnetic spectrum. While it is true that infrared has less energy than visible light, when we say that, we're talking about individual photons. However, in this experiment, there are more photons with the infrared. Another factor to consider, is that what the thermometer is measuring isn't the light itself, but is the surface that's absorbing the light."

"Ah," I said, nodding.

"I'm also confused about the infrared waves themselves. I can't see them, but supposedly they can help see invisible things too, right?"

"Infrared light can also be used to see the differences in molecules." Ed said. "Differences at the molecular level are no longer visible to the naked eye. Do you understand why plastics absorb and reflect infrared differently?"

"Umm... Not really. I mean I have a guess..."

"Let's hear it!"

I blinked. "Okay... Back in the summer, I got a chemistry kit, and I noticed that different polymers' basic structure had different shapes, even though they were made out of the same elements. So if they absorb and reflect infrared light different-ly, I'm guessing that maybe the shapes have something to do with it?"

He smiled. "Absolutely! Differ-ent types of plastics are bonded and held together in different ways. The angles of these bonds cause the whole object to ab-sorb and reflect wavelengths in different ways. Recycling com-panies use infrared because the differences in the mid-infrared region are especially clear. But you can still see differences in near or far infrared."

Testing different LEDs to determine the best wavelength for fluroscence of microplastic dyes

He added, "Spectroscopes take in all the light shining on them, break it down into different wavelengths, and then digitize the signal and display it. They can either shine light onto an object and see how it absorbs the light, or look at the natural lights reflecting from the objects."

I tried to write it all down in my notebook as fast as possible.

"Does that mean I could use something like... I dunno... are there infrared LEDs? Can I shine the light onto the plastics and then... somehow detect how they reflect?"

"Maaaybe," he said smiling, "We have infrared LEDs in the supply cabinet. Take some home to play with. And take a webcam too!"

"Huh," I replied. So I went home and built a circuit that allowed me to shine infrared light from a single LED onto my samples.

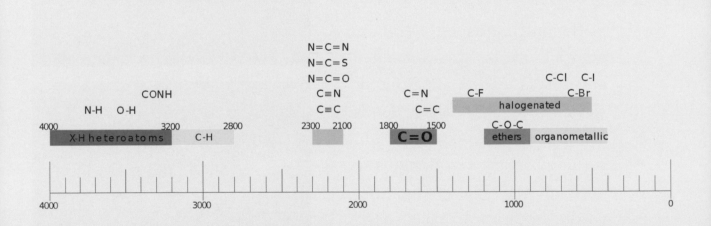

IR spectroscopy sample (unit: nm)
This chart shows where on the spectrum different chemical bonds absorb infrared light. By studying patterns of absorption, it's possible to figure out a lot about the structure of a molecule.

Chapter 12

Somewhere Over The Rainbow

As I nodded off to sleep that night, I started designing ROV models in my head. I narrowed in on three main ideas.

My first plan was to attach some sort of suctioning device to my ROV, grab samples from different locations, and then deliver them to be analyzed in a lab. The idea seemed simple. No complicated electronics. On the other hand, collecting data would take forever. Even if I carted a truckful of samples to a lab each day, that still wouldn't make a dent on researching even 1% of the ocean floor.

The second method I considered was to suck up sand from the ocean floor and analyze the samples within the ROV itself. This way, I could do the testing in-situ, meaning right in place. However, this design would be complicated, and would therefore have a lot of places where it could potentially go wrong. Not to mention, there was a slight chance that animals might get stuck inside the device.

The final method would be to create a machine that could examine the samples right where they lay on the ocean floor. The design would be simple enough, since it would avoid the hassle of sucking the samples up. This way, the ROV wouldn't cause harm to animals. The only downside I could see was that the electronics might get wet.

As I was just about to sleep, I settled on Method Three. Luckily, I still remembered that by the next morning when I woke to the sound of my mom calling to me to get ready. I grabbed a pencil and jotted down my thoughts from the night before.

My door blasted open. "Hey, are we going or not?" my dad asked, standing alongside one of his friends, holding fishing poles in his hand. Hmm, I thought to myself, looks like a bigger trip than Boston Harbor.

"Where are we heading?" I asked.

"Didn't your mom tell you? Fishing on the Cape followed by lobsters and clams!" His smile was huge. My family is really big on seafood. That may be one of the reasons they're so supportive of my interest in cleaning up the ocean.

My family had already cooked up breakfast to go and loaded up the car. Even Andy was already sitting in the back seat waiting for me. I grabbed my sea glass collecting backpack and gear and ran to the car with fresh ideas buzzing around in my head. It would be a long drive.

I must have fallen asleep quickly, because the next thing I

remember was my mom calling out, "We're here!"

In a few minutes, my family and friends had marched off to fish and find lunch at Wellfleet Bay. Meanwhile, Andy and I strolled in the muddy flats near the wharf. I kneeled down to pick up some sea-shells when a tall, old, bearded local fisherman wearing a dirty, shred-ded Patriots hat and a camouflage jacket called over to me.

"Don't be picking up any of those oysters!" he yelled in a thick Boston accent.

I jumped. "Why? Are they pollut-ed or something?"

"Heck no, these days these are the clean-est shellfish in New England, probably the whole East Coast! But they belong to my friends, you know. So many tourists come out here and steal our clams and oysters."

His equally rugged-looking fishing buddy chimed in. "People are harvesting so many oysters, the ones we have left seem to get smaller every year." The buddy turned to me. "That's why you need a permit for that, little girl. You don't want to go to jail, do you?"

A little frightened, I answered, "I wasn't trying to take any of your oysters—just some

Cape Cod oysters. I didn't take any of these, just stones and seaglasses.

empty shells and maybe some rocks and stuff."

"Well, in that case, knock yourself out. Just don't be skipping rocks or throwing anything in the water to scare all the schoolies away." Schoolies and stripers are local terms for striped bass, I later found out.

I turned back to the first fisherman. "Hey, did the Harbor used to be dirty before?"

Several men laughed. "Of course! Haven't you heard that old song 'Love that dirty water—Boston, you're my home?' The harbor practically stank. You could find cancers growing on the livers of fish we caught."

Another man wearing a striped shirt said, "There are a lot more sharks all around here than there were twenty years ago! Even a lot of giant Great Whites now too! It's like that old movie *Jaws* is coming true."

"Why would there be more sharks?" I asked.

"Well, they started cleaning up Boston Harbor a few decades ago and some of the life came back, like the harbor seals. The sharks eat the seals whenever they're not eating little girls like you who get too close to the water. Haha."

I backed away from the man wearing the striped shirt, who was still guffawing at his own humor, and turned to the others. "So it was dirty before.... What an amazing change!"

"It's not perfect," a bald man in a torn shirt told me. "They did a great job cleaning up the sewage and chemicals and things, but I think there's still a lot of regular trash out there seems to be affecting everything. Used to be you could catch all kinds of fish. Quincy used to be the flounder capital of the world. Not anymore.

Trash and too many people fishing out here!"

I knew that there was something worse than just trash. Somewhere over the rainbow of visible light, UV was making the problem even worse. It breaks down trash like plastics, which are photodegradable, not biodegradable, turning the plastics into microplastics. But on the other side of the rainbow, maybe we could use infrared to identify those pieces of plastics.

"There are a lot of other problems now," the bald man said. "Look at the baby sea turtles."

"Baby sea turtles?" I echoed.

"Haven't you heard? Thousands of sea turtles getting lost and washing up on our shores! Way too far north."

The man wearing the baseball cap chimed in, "Yeah, people are saying that it's because of climate change."

Just then, one of the men caught a small fish, and their attention drifted. Andy and I strolled back to rejoin the others, who were plowing into their clams. I thought about what I had learned.

It started to make sense to me. The ocean is such a vast and complicated place; lots of different factors are at play, causing marine life to shift over time. Pollution, climate change, fishing, complicated interactions within the food chain—still, I felt somehow encouraged. Cleaning up Boston Harbor was an immense accomplishment. To think that people managed to clean up something that large! Sure, it took decades, but it meant that we can do something big. We've done it before.

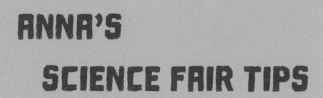

ANNA'S
SCIENCE FAIR TIPS

REACH OUT TO SOME EXPERTS IN THEIR FIELDS. There are tons of people in every single field. Most of them are very nice, and will hear you out as you describe your project, and chances are, they might give you pretty helpful advice as well!

Chapter 13

Digging Deeper Into The Topic

At home, I started researching what was happening to the sea turtles around Cape Cod. I learned how "cold stunning" affects turtles, especially the endangered Ridley's Kemp turtles, when they get confused and disoriented due to changing weather patterns and ocean currents.

The fact that the ocean shifts around a lot might make my cleanup tasks even harder. It was something to think about. I wanted to learn more. After searching, I learned about a person who was very involved in local marine life rescues—a charismatic and cheery woman named Carol 'Krill' Carson.

We started a correspondence, and she invited me to come see one of her latest advanced technology projects, where she was mapping nests of diamondback terrapin turtles. These turtles have a problem with nest sites disappearing because of construction, pollution and other factors.

Krill does her rescues on Cape Cod. When I visited her, she led me down to the beach, barefoot. She seemed so happy to be by the ocean. I was amazed to see her run across the shoreline at low tide, still barefoot.

"Doesn't that hurt? You must have feet made of pure steel!"

She laughed. "Oh, I'm used to it by now. In the beginning, it did really hurt, though."

Rescued turtle

We then walked around, looking for areas where there might be turtle eggs.

"Why are you looking for these eggs?" I asked.

"We want to be able to keep these turtles safe. One of the best methods to do that is to understand where the turtles are laying their eggs, and why they're laying them there," she explained.

I nodded.

We walked to a clear patch in the grassy field, and Krill and her team of researchers started setting up a giant aerial drone.

"What's that drone for?"

Snapping the battery of the drone on, Krill answered, "This is used to map this area. When we set the drone off into the air it'll be able to create a diagram showing this entire area. Then, when we know where the turtle eggs are, we can place each site onto the maps, and when we come back every few weeks, we can track them."

I was awed by how her team was using engineering and aerial mapping to try to solve an environmental problem. Krill told me they were even using drones to collect whale spit.

It occurred to me that I could apply spatial mapping to my ROV as well. It'd be great if I could map all the microplastics on the ocean floor onto a gigantic ocean floor map. That might be the way to find the great underwater microplastic patch under the ocean, which I just knew must be there somewhere.

At the next Make Day, a group of students hunched over what looked like a board game.

"Oooh, that's cool! What are you making that for?" I asked one of the girls.

"It's sort of like a matching game. You have to find the correct order of the different wooden chips. If you order

Carol 'Krill' Carson and her team explain how they use their drones to create a spatial map of where the turtle eggs are.

them correctly, then the light on top will turn green."

"Wow! So how did you make it?" I'd played with snap circuits before, but this looked different.

Cut PCB

She flipped the board around, saying, "I etched this design for my own chip onto this piece of cardboard so I could create my own circuit. Do you want to know how?"

"Definitely!" That's the great thing about makers: we all teach one another.

"Okay, so I first got this piece of copper, right? Then I attached a light-sensitive material to the copper plate." She demonstrated what she meant. A light-sensitive sheet could be bonded to the copper-coated PCB blank using a thermal laminator. "For the next step, there are multiple different ways you can do this. You can use a sharpie, or you can print a copy on transparent paper with the pattern in reverse, and tape it onto the light-sensitive material." She showed me how either way would block light from reaching certain parts of the light-sensitive sheet. "Then you expose your board

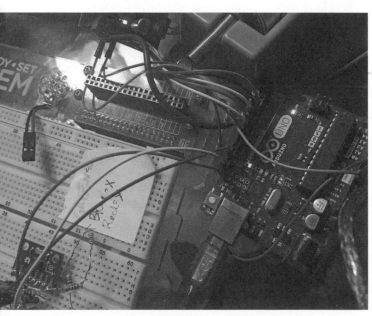

Breadboarding various electronics prior to installing them in the ROV

to sunlight. The part that's sensitive to light and isn't covered up will harden and stay behind, forming a sort of stencil. After that, you dip the board into sodium hydroxide, which is basically drain cleaner. That helps wash away the rest of the unneeded photoresist, the region that didn't get exposed to sunlight. Don't worry about the part under the sun—that area is already bonded to the circuit board. Then, once you rinse your board, you dip it into ferric chloride, which etches the copper."

After she showed me how to make a circuit, I worked on making my own circuit for my infrared detection system. I needed infrared light from my ROV to fall evenly on parts of the ocean floor it was exploring. So I arranged all of the infrared LEDs into a circular pattern and put them on a raised surface.

Now the light spread evenly, solving most of the problems I had with the old circuit, which only shined light on one side of the samples, casting long shadows. I was creating my own circuit!

Now I could take infrared photos, and I could analyze a photo by collecting data—how dark or bright a point seemed under certain light—from each pixel point on a photo. But doing that was incredibly tedious. So I decided to program the task.

Testing the LEDs to take pictures utilizing the infrared detection system

I had been learning the computer programming language Python for some time. But now that I was trying to program something all my own, I found coding a lot harder than when I was doing exercises someone else gave me.

Before, I had coded a few games and websites. But coding images and adjusting them to show certain features well was a completely different experience for me. For one, I had to download a different library or set of miniprograms to use, one that was new to me. I had to keep searching up what to do more than I'd like to admit. Before this experience, I didn't know that there were so many possible ways for a program NOT to work.

In the end, though, my program worked perfectly to identifying the plastics on a petri dish! It scanned entire photos quickly. The best part? In the past, with me just picking a few points, I was only able to work with the raw data in the form of numbers. However, the computer was able to take that data and put it into an enhanced photo so I could visualize the results. That was when I first started to wonder if artificial intelligence (AI) could eventually teach the computer to identify plastics all by itself. But I knew that was too much for me to tackle right away.

The picture was great.

Connecting the infrared system to a Raspberry Pi to take automatic pictures.

It clearly highlighted the differences between plastics and other things you might find in the ocean, like sand, seashells, and metals. Still, I was only working with known pieces of plastic. I wanted to see how my system would handle unknown microplastics. I planned to collect

Ocean sand microscope

some from the beach, but because the days were getting colder, I also wanted to create my own synthetic samples.

ANNA'S
SCIENCE FAIR TIPS

KEEP A WORKING LOG OF YOUR PROJECT. It doesn't matter how big or small the event is—as long as it has something to do with your project, you should write it down in a notebook. This notebook will serve as your journal, and judges can use it to see how your project has progressed over time. It's interesting, for the people who view your project, to see how you've made every single decision that impacts your project.

Chapter 14

The Ocean Simulation Machine

One day, my parents took us all to a good spot in our neighborhood for a walk. I took off with Andy at my side. He drifted behind, and when I turned around I saw that he was a good forty feet back, sniffing at something in the sand.

"Andy!" I called.

He turned his head around to look at me, seeming to say, *Can't you tell I'm doing something?* before turning back to his task. Curious, I walked down to see what he'd found.

It was a broken CD player. My eyes widened. I couldn't believe someone would throw something like that away. There were so many parts I could use!

Because my parents were facing the other way, I saw my chance. I sprinted to the house and put the CD player next to a bush. Then I walked back to Andy.

"Good boy!"

He licked my face.

Later, after I finished walking Andy, I retrieved the CD player again and brought it into the house.

"Why on earth would you bring in a piece of trash?" my mom asked in a scandalized voice.

I put on a pleading face. "I want to make an ocean simulation machine. If I find the correct parts on this CD player with enough voltage, then maybe I can make the part on the middle spin and simulate the motion of the currents. Hopefully, my simulation machine will grind down sea glass fragments like the ones I picked up from the beach. Maybe it will even make rounded microplastic beads the way natural forces do."

My mom sighed. "Can you at least wipe it off before you take it to your room?"

After that, I got to work. First, I spun the CD parts around, just to see if the machine was rusted or not. Then, I needed to find where to get the power from. I remembered my dad taught me years ago how to use a multimeter, which can tell how much power is still in a battery.

The motor I wanted to use was rated at 5 volts. The circuit part of the CD player was a sea of resistors and capacitors and transformers and circuitry, and I carefully, step by step, touched the multimeter probes to various combinations of metal leads to see which had the right power level.. 24 volts... 12 volts... 8 volts... no, that wouldn't work... 3 volts... 4 volts... Finally 5.0 volts!

After I finally found a combination with just the right amount of power, I moved to the next step. I got two empty plastic water bottles and cut one of them up to make a kind of nest or clamp that could secure the second bottle into place. I put this holder in the middle of the CD player. Then I used a blender to mash up pieces of plastics. I wanted to create smaller, potentially microplastic-sized pieces, like those YouTube videos where blenders destroy just about anything, such as phones and spoons. Finally, I filled the second bottle with water, sand, shells, sea glass, and most importantly, tiny pieces of plastic.

Ocean water sampling at Boston Harbour

A close up of the microplastics created from the blender

When I turned my contraption on, the water bottle started to rotate. It was working perfectly! I decided that every two weeks, I would take a sample from the bottle contents and examine it under the microscope. I wanted to see how my pieces of plastic abraded with all of these different materials scratching them. I also wanted to take a look at how the plastics appeared under my infrared detection system.

But by the next morning, the machine had come to a halt. I frowned. The cord seemed to be connected. I spun the water bottle for a bit. That triggered the entire machine to work again. But what was wrong with it? I couldn't keep checking it throughout the day—I had school.

I tried putting a piece of cardboard under the part that was supporting the top of the water bottle, so it wouldn't get dragged down. In a couple of hours, I checked on my spinner again. It seemed to be working. I sighed. Crisis averted for now.

Checking the Ocean Simulation machine to see how my tiny plastics are doing.

Chapter 15

Engineering Design Process

I t was time to focus on the underwater vehicle itself. I had ideas for it, now I needed to implement them. I scrounged around my basement looking for pieces of spare PVC.

I nearly cackled when I saw a large pile of PVC tubes left over from a past renovation.

I laid out the shape on the floor and started building, looking at the pictures of Nereid and Jason that I had printed out. Both looked cube-shaped. A cube would be easy enough to make, right? I arranged the

Assembling my ROV, trying to create a shape that would be able to maneuver well in the ocean

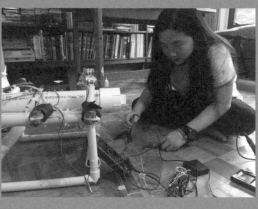

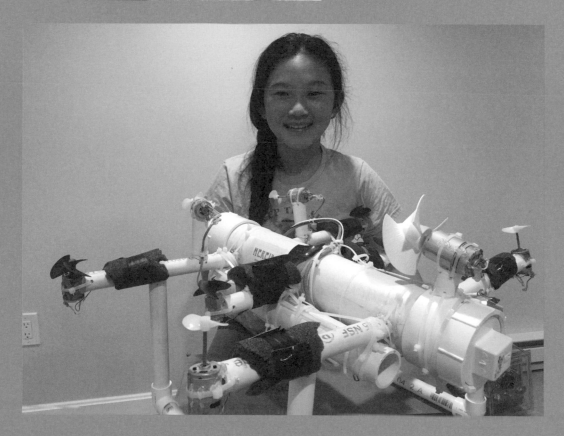

structure to form something I was satisfied with, and then glued the pieces together. Huh. That was pretty easy, I thought.

I connected two of my motors on the top side, on parallel edges. Both faced forwards, slightly tilted so they could move the ROV left and right.

In place of my detection system, because I hadn't really created one yet, I put a webcam that was around the size which I thought the detection system would be. I tried attaching it to one of the sides, but it kept sliding down. I bit my lip. Maybe I needed some support on the bottom to keep the detection system on. Not to mention, I had another motor to add too!

I cut the sides on the bottom and added a cross in the middle. After doing this, attaching the separate parts was much easier. I set the motor in the middle, pitched at a 45° angle to move the ROV both up and forward at the same time. The webcam faced the front more, to look at the ground ahead.

Now that I had installed my navigation system, I wanted to test it right away, so I headed for bathtub.

I knew that my mom would be furious if she knew I was testing my ROV, no matter how clean, in the bathtub where she bathes. That's why I decided to lock the door.

The space wasn't big enough for much maneuvering, but at least I could see my ROV move. All of the basic functions seemed to be working. However, it took a long time for the heavy ROV to slowly inch upward, and it had a clear tendency to turn upside down.

My test demonstrated two things I needed to do—arrange more motors so the ROV didn't flip over, and find something that would make the ROV neutrally buoyant. Fortunately, I knew where to get all the materials that I needed—from that same recent house renovation, we had a good supply of foam insulation materials.

The only problem? How to escape the bathroom without being discovered. Looking around, I hastily shoved the ROV into the cabinet and walked out of the room. I walked in a very leisurely, unconcerned fashion to the basement, found the foam I needed, and scurried back. Andy looked at me, seemingly trying to ask, *What on Earth are you doing?*

In the bathroom, I dropped the foam onto the countertop and breathed a sigh of relief. I put the ROV in the water again and wrapped foam around it. Sometimes, the ROV still stayed on the bottom, sometimes, I went a bit overboard with the foam, and it floated to the top! Even worse, sometimes the ROV tilted because I put more foam on one side of the ROV than the other. But eventually I achieved something like neutral buoyancy. The ROV hovered.

But once I dumped out all the water from the PVC pipes and made sure everything was waterproof, my ROV was too light. I didn't want to mess with my careful balance, and the foam was tightly attached, so I left the bathroom again. This time, I was searching for something heavy to weigh down the machine. In the garage, I finally found what I was looking for—some old window counterweights.

Testing the buoyancy of the ROV in a bathtub

I shoved the weights in place and capped the pipes as tightly as I could.

In the beginning, it was fine. The ROV had even started to hover in the middle of the water! I was just about to do a happy dance, when I noticed something weird drifting from the cap...

The water was turning darker and darker.

I knelt down to get a better look. I gasped. The iron counter-weights were rusty! As I hurriedly drained the bathtub, and took out my ROV, I prayed that the leaking rust wouldn't permanently stain the floor or bathtub.

Then the scratching on the door started. My heart skipped a beat as I heard footsteps approaching, "Andy, what's going on? There's nothing in the bathroom!" my mom cooed, laughing, "See?"

Oh no.

My mom tried to open the door. It was locked.

"Anna? Are you in there?" she yelled.

"...Yes?"

"Well, open up!"

"I'm... using the toilet! Hold on!"

"Anna... I know you're not. What do you have in the bathtub?"

My face dropped, and slowly, I opened the door.

Her hands flew to her mouth. "Anna! What was the one rule I gave you when you started this project?"

"...To not make a mess?" I said, quietly.

"Get out, clean up everything!" she screeched, shoving the

wet ROV into my arms and draining the tub.

The good thing was that I already knew what I needed to fix. The bad thing was once I fixed it, I had no means of testing it. I would have to come up with another way.

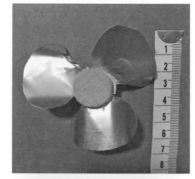

In order to get more power for my motor, I would need a different shape, and maybe even a different material to give it more thrust. But what material could I use? I set down the soda can that I was drinking from. If I were to test what shapes would work the best, I would need something flexible enough to bend, but hard enough so after I was done, it would retain its shape.

I eyed the soda can again.

A few hours later, my parents found me using epoxy to glue two different layers of metal from the soda can propellers together. I had already cut out the same shape multiple times. For some of them, I barely twisted the blade. But for others, I twisted it as much as I could without breaking it.

Once I finished, and they all

Testing propeller designs and adding propellers

dried, I attached the propellers to a motor. Right before I put the motor in a bucket filled with water, however, I almost quit my experiment. I looked up, and I saw the ceiling fan. It was almost completely flat. Why would someone design fans to be flat, if that weren't the most efficient way of pushing air?

Still, I decided to move forward with my test just for the fun of it. That was a good idea, because it turns out, my theory was wrong. The most flat propeller barely pushed the water at all compared to the one that was really twisted and angled.

Then, I created an online 3D model of the propeller I was looking for. I wanted to use that to see if any hardware store would be able to recreate it or have a similar looking pro- peller. Or... perhaps... I sent my friend Cecily a text message.

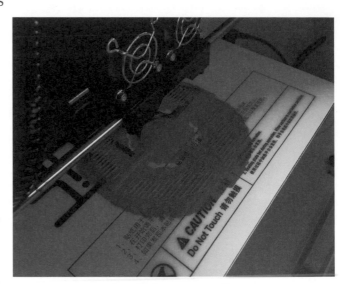

3-D printing a propeller

A couple of hours later, she sent a text back to me

"Ok! Sure! Knock yourself out. This 3D printer isn't any good just sitting on top of my desk! Besides, there's still a chance Amanda might take it!!!"

I laughed at my friend's words. Amanda and Cecily were sib- lings who were always getting into fights. Once Amanda de- stroyed Cecily's tape recorder in a fit of rage when Cecily left on a trip. Now whenever she went anywhere, Cecily entrusted some of her dearest possessions to her friends to "protect them from

Amanda's temper tantrums."

"Thank you so muucchhh!!"

Once I got the printer, I downloaded my designs onto it. I wanted to test two designs, one with three blades and the other with four, to see if there were any differences in efficiency.

What I didn't expect was how long the 3D printing was going to take.

After an hour, the base of one propeller still wasn't finished yet. It was so frustrating. So I just stood there and stared at my ROV. I always like to jazz up whatever I create. My books have personalized bookmarks; my plant pots have decorations that identify them. My ROV needed some special look. I decided to add LEDs to all the motors. Once I was done, I felt like the ROV had a more personal touch to it. I made sure all the added LEDs were

blue, white, or green, as a way of showing what the word Nereid really means in Ancient Greek—a spirit of saltwater.

However, in order to test my new contraption, I had to wait until the next Make Day, because my mom had banned me from using the bathtub.

Testing propeller in water

Chapter 16

Starting All Over Again

After a few days of waiting, Make Day finally came. I was practically bouncing off the walls in excitement.

Once I got into the lab, I immediately went for the inflatable pool. They sometimes have it there for students to test their "things." It was time to test my new ROV along with the neutral buoyancy.

In the beginning, all was well, but soon, I realized that my ROV just simply wasn't maneuverable enough. It almost couldn't accelerate at all.

Mr. Ed walked by. "Still working on your project?"

"Yeah. The ROV just doesn't seem to be moving as much as I'd like it to," I said. "I didn't want it to be a race car, but I also don't want it to be like in some slow-motion movie."

He laughed, "Well, you could keep adding motors and

propellers. Or, you could just increase the arms and place the propellers farther out to get more maneuverability. A cube may not be the best shape. If you need a camera always facing the bottom, then you should create something that has a clear, defining top and bottom."

I nodded. What he said did make a lot of sense. I sighed and took my ROV out of the pool. Maybe, in spite of Jason and Nereid, a cube wasn't the best shape for an ROV like this.

Instead of blindly reaching for the PVC tubes to build again when I got home, I chose to design my improved ROV with a CAD (computer-assisted design) program. This time, I designed an extremely complicated machine, which had a lot of extra parts, most of which were unnecessary. The next day, when I looked at my design, I immediately knew I had forgotten one of the rules: keep it simple. I thought back to a book I had read, *The Boy Who Harnessed the Wind.* I thought about it for nights after reading it. I was struck by the thought that people who don't have resources become resourceful and make do, while people who have an abundance of resources just waste them.

I needed to become resourceful. And thus, I started redesigning again.

ANNA DU R.O.V. 1.0 SYSTEM OVERVIEW

ACCELEROMETER/GYROSCOPE-DRIVEN MOTOR CONTROL SYSTEM FOR PITCH/ROLL LEVELING

NAVIGATION SCREEN

TETHERED R.O.V.

12 V BATTERY

OR

NAVIGATION & L.E.D. CONTROLLER

WATERPROOF I.R. CAM & MULTI-L.E.D. SYSTEM

DC POWER SUPPLY

LAPTOP FOR ANALYSIS OF I.R. WEBCAM IMAGES

TARGET SAMPLES - EITHER IN LAB OR UNDERWATER

Here's a basic diagram of my first ROV system

When I was laying out my pieces on the ground of the living room, I suddenly heard frantic panting, along with rushed sounds of paws scratching the floor. My dad was chasing Andy, no doubt because he had done something wrong. I realized what was happening a second too late.

Andy rushed to the living room and jumped on top of my laid-out structure, scattering what I had balanced so precariously.

"Andy!" I complained.

My dad winced, saying, "Sorry about that. I'll make sure he stays away from here."

I pursed my lips. Good thing I had an online version of what my design should look like, so I wouldn't have to start all over again with only memory to guide me. I was pretty happy that my family were starting to take my project seriously (with the exception of James), and no one was yelling at me for messing up the living room floor. Instead, they were trying to give me the space I needed.

This version had a lot more loose parts that couldn't be stuck together with only PVC connectors. Once I finished my layout, I used PVC glue to stick the pieces together. I spent a long time holding the pieces in place and positioning random objects such as books and lamps to support the ROV. I was determined not to let my structure fall apart in the middle of the glue drying.

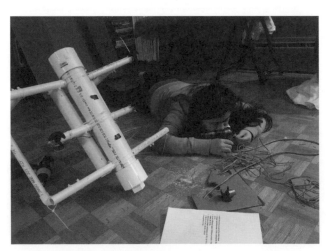
Rebuilding my ROV on the living room floor

The next day, however, as soon as I took the support objects away, the joints started cracking. I tried to smoosh the pieces together again, but soon, the structure completely fell apart. Maybe I wasn't using enough glue. I redid everything, this time making sure to slather on the glue. The next day, I added a second layer of glue. This time I was sure I could keep the whole thing standing.

One more day and I was proven wrong. When I took off the materials supporting it, the ROV cracked, and when I tugged on it slightly, pieces ripped off.

I didn't know what to do. Clearly, adding more glue wasn't helping the process at all. I felt like screaming and pulling my hair out. Taking my homework, I huffed and sat down on my table. We were getting more and more homework, and I was beginning to fall behind. Time for a break from my ROV!

Using a glue gun to attach the joints

A couple days later, my school began our "nature week," where we spent whole days outside in the forest. In place of our regular classes, like Algebra and Grammar, we focused on biology and survival skills. We built things with rope and learned about edible foods.

Other times, we had informational classes. That's where inspiration struck one day.

During a class on the digestive system, my teacher mentioned that the stomach uses two methods to break food down: chemical and physical. My mind flashed back to my ROV. I was only using a chemical binding process—the glue. On my previous version, I'd used a physical approach—connectors. What would happen if I got back to something physical?

When I got home, I scrambled to search for something to hold the ROV together. I looked through all of my drawers filled with supplies and thought about each potential option. Nuts and bolts? Clamps? Rubber bands? That's when I found it. A giant drawer filled with... cable ties!

Perfect!

I drilled holes in different parts of the PVC piping, then looped the cable ties through the holes, making sure to secure them tightly. Finally, I added PVC glue to make the structure extra

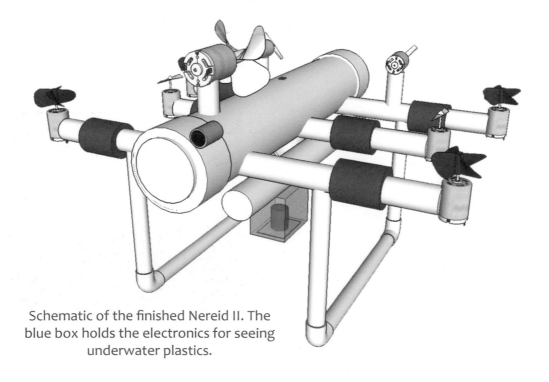

Schematic of the finished Nereid II. The blue box holds the electronics for seeing underwater plastics.

secure. When the glue dried, I tried to pull the ROV apart. This time, the ROV stayed together.

This is something that I've noticed in recent years—sometimes I can be working on a project for weeks, and not come up with a solution. Then, I take a few days off or work on a small side-project. Once I return, I always come up with some different approaches. Sometimes, a little time away can lead to a new solution.

ANNA'S
SCIENCE FAIR TIPS

SCIENCE FAIRS TAKE A LOT OF TIME—BE SURE NOT TO UNDERESTIMATE THIS FACT. Make sure you leave yourself plenty of time to build your boards, and be sure to practice your science fair discussions with others. The most important part of a science fair is your "elevator pitch" to judges, and then how knowledgeably you talk with them once you've lured them in!

Chapter 17

Time For Testing

The next day, I went to the beach with my new ROV in tow. I was ready to test it. As soon as I got there, I realized my first problem—I'd forgotten to bring water-proof shoes.

I was wearing sneakers. They were water repellant, but as soon as water got in, you could expect soggy shoes for a week at least. When I asked my mom if I was allowed to go in, she shook her head.

So I found a workaround.

I could use a stick to prod the ROV into the water! Once it was partially submerged, I could then direct the ROV to move itself deeper. But as soon as I managed to poke the ROV into the ocean, I realized my problem. Because the ocean has more particulates, higher density, and more current, the propellers on my ROV would have to be stronger than in a pool.

The ROV didn't have enough power to move! I could barely see the propellers turning, and sometimes they stopped altogether. There was only one silver lining to my very dark, very sad cloud. Those LEDs I had originally added for decoration helped me track where the ROV was underwater! But they didn't help the ROV move. Dejectedly, I tugged my contraption back onto the sand. There was nothing more I could do at the beach.

When I got home, I knew that I had to add a much more reliable power supply. I searched the house for another source of power. I searched everywhere, but I just couldn't find what I was looking for. In the end, I asked my dad for help.

"Do you know if there's any source of power that could make my ROV move? I mean, you saw how terrible it was today, right?" I said.

He shook his head. "Right now, we don't have anything in the house, but I'm sure we can order it. But do you need anything else? Let's order everything you might need in one go."

I nodded. My dad went online to search for power supplies. In the end, we settled on a 12-volt lawnmower battery and some marine sealants.

Both objects finally arrived a few days later. I almost cried in relief—patience was never my strong suit.

When I first tested the new battery on the ROV, a propeller flew off, ricocheting everywhere—onto the ceiling, wall, and against the opposite wall, before finally dropping onto the floor. I slammed my hand on the power off button. Good thing I was wearing safety goggles and other protection gear. I mean, I like science and engineering, but not enough to lose an eyeball for it.

I realized that this meant the propellers weren't connected well enough. After that, once I put marine sealant on the shafts, I hot-glued that propeller as much as I could to make sure something like that wouldn't happen again. Still, the next time I tested it, I made sure to pull out the tether as far as it could to so I could sit far away. No more propellers flew off!

The next time I went to the beach, I was feeling a lot more confident. I was sure that I had prepared everything, maybe even over-prepared. I brought a lot more supplies this time—duct tape, cable ties, foam insulants, everything I could think of to prepare the ROV. I even remembered to bring rainboots!

I changed locations from the sandy beach onto a rocky hill which was closer to the water. As I predicted, there were a lot of buoyancy issues. The ROV kept sinking, so I had to add pieces of foam onto all the arms. My contraption also kept tipping, sometimes even flipping over completely. One of the propellers had been knocked and started wobbling. Once I got home, I would need to fix that.

Then it started raining. Not just the usual small, ignorable rain, but the pouring kind. The kind of storm that could leave you feeling like you just stood in a cold shower for an hour with all your clothes on. Which was pretty close to reality, actually.

"Dang it!"

It was only then that I realized that I hadn't actually thought of everything. I had waterproofed all the motors and sealed up the navigation system connecting to the tether, but when it started pouring I saw that I had forgotten to waterproof the most important thing—the control box, which was made of cardboard.

Whirrrrrr.... Zap.

My motors all came to a stop, followed by some sort of electric shock sound. I guess that was it. The experiment was officially over.

I tried to poke my ROV with a long nearby stick to see if it would move, to no avail. But as I lunged toward the machine, my foot landed on slick, seaweed-covered rocks. I tried to catch myself, but—

Splash.

Yep, that was the sound of everything below my waistline ending up in the freezing cold Atlantic Ocean, during wintertime. And I had cut my hand on a mussel shell on the way down.

"Mo-o-o-m!"

Yep, that was the sound of me freaking out and shouting for help. Fortunately, several people came to my call and helped to grab my stuff. We ran back to the car, where Andy jumped out to greet me, quickly getting wetter than I was. I got in the car and

Testing the ROV at the beach

turned my seat warmer up full blast. Andy cuddled up to me like a smelly, cold, wet blanket all the way home. I can say definitively that this was the most uncomfortable moment of field work during my whole project.

I learned quite a few lessons that day. Not just about engineering, but also about bringing an extra pair of clothes in the car!

After Andy and I dried out under some nice clean blankets near the heater and drank hot cocoa, I redid the control box. This time, I re-made it in wood with laminated navigation markers and more robust switches and wiring. The improved version would definitely be able to handle a little rain.

I designed a homegrown relay as a personal experiment to understand more about how to isolate circuits so that the navigation system and the control of the motors could be operated at entierly different voltages and currents. I did this because my motors needed more power in order to operate in a turbulent ocean environment without disturbing the sensitive micro controllers in my main system. With this new feature, my ROV can now sail more powerfully and reliably.

As Thomas Edison once said, "I have not failed 10,000 times— I've successfully found 10,000 ways that will not work."

Testing new wood box battery controller

Chapter 18

The More The Merrier

As I sat on the floor testing my new and improved control box, my dad brought in a package. I ripped it open. It was what I'd seen some students using last Make Day—a book of Arduino projects to make. I had recently been playing with my Arduino kit, and I wanted to try some new designs.

I flipped through the pages and I saw just what I was looking for—a section on building an accelerometer gyroscope. That would let me know the position and direction of my ROV underwater. However, the more I read, the more confused I got.

Arduino setup

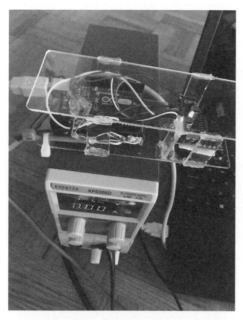

Accelerometer

In the end, I gave up reading and just started building the accelerometer gyroscope-driven balancing system. There were some materials that I didn't have, and the instructions were designed for two motors to be connected, instead of one, so I had to tweak the overall design for hours to get it to work correctly. It took me days. In my confusion, due to the sheer multitude of wires with similar colors sticking out everywhere, connected to alligator clips that were connected to other alligator clips, I often connected something to the wrong place. Worse yet, wires could come undone with the slightest jostle.

I can't count how many times I had to re-start the whole wiring process from scratch. During this process I learned to start labeling wires and other parts of my system. Otherwise, it's easy to get lost. I suppose this was why MIT's motto is *mens et manus*—mind and hands. Years of school, textbooks and standardized tests may have some sort of meaning, I suppose. But you simply can't beat doing something with your hands, if you want to learn something the right way.

Testing out the motor controller and accelerometer/gyroscope to see how well it balances the ROV

A couple of hours after I finished, I found myself on the sofa, talking to James… again.

"Hey, butterfly, still trying to be a happy-go-lucky, world-saving saint?" he sneered.

I huffed. "I told you to stop calling me butterfly!" I described my wonderful machine.

He remained skeptical. "Sounds cute, but I doubt it really works. How can you prove it's actually identifying plastics? It's probably calling any old small thing it comes across a plastic."

In the following days, still seething from my cousin's words, I set out to prove him wrong.

In science fairs, one of the most important things, even when doing an engineering project, is to test controls vs. variables. I planned to test my own known samples of plastics vs. other particles, such as wood, seashells, sand, metals, and other plastics. I planned to collect lots of data to see if my system could effectively differentiate synthetic polymers from other things.

I also normalized my data (which means I found a way to make the data comparable to each other) and scaled them. That way, I could use my results to create a color map of an area the ROV scanned, showing the areas with highest and lowest absorptions. By varying and testing the samples, I effectively made both an engineering design project and a traditional science experiment at the same time. I hoped future judges would be impressed with the cross-disciplinary aspect of my approach.

To double check the system, I still had the jar filled with samples from my ocean simulation machine. It had been a solid six weeks since I started, and maybe some plastics had already turned into microplastics. I was ready to use my samples.

I realized that to double check the accuracy of my system, I didn't need an ocean environment. I could use more sophisticated methods in a lab. So I turned again to something I'd learned about early on—Nile Red dye. I found what I was looking for in an article in *Nature*. It turns out that if plastics are treated with Nile Red dye, you can look at them under a filter lens of a specific wavelength, and they fluoresce brightly versus other particles.

Using Nile Red dye to confirm the presence of plastics in samples

The good part was, the website listed the materials and procedures I needed to follow. The bad part was, some of the materials would need parental supervision. I also would need a fluorescent microscope to do this—something mostly found in labs. I knew my mom had a friend who worked in a chemistry department at a nearby university, so I begged my mom to set up an appointment.

Professor Selina was even nicer than I expected. In fact, as soon as my mom and I entered the lab, she gave each of us a big hug.

Sample vials containing microplastics and fluorescent dye

"Anna, your mother has told me so much about your project! What are you planning to do today? I'll try my best to help you!"

"Thank you so much! I'd like to submerge pieces of plastic in different concentrations of Nile Red Dye. Then, I'd like to use a specific wavelength of blue under an orange filter to try and identify plastics," I said, my voice slowly gaining confidence as I spoke more and more.

She nodded. "I think we can do that."

And so we got to work. As we worked, she quizzed me on my knowledge.

"Do you know how Nile Red Dye works?"

"I read that it was a li-po-phi-lic dye which only attaches to certain types of organic molecules, making it good for identifying plastics," I said, slowly pronouncing the word.

"Yeah! That's right!"

Once we were done, I looked at the microscope. I noticed that freshly cut plastics had brighter sides than the ones that had been abraded from the ocean simulation machine.

Putting together an LED connected with a potentiometer to control the wavelength, so I can see what wavelength allows Nile Red dye's fluorescence to show up the best

But that good mood was squashed as soon as I got the results for the color mapping system—my identifications were only a bit over half accurate. I pursed my lips. It looked like James was right. This was definitely not accurate enough. I expressed my disappointment to Professor Selina.

She said, "Hey, you know, one of my students worked on a project similar to yours. Not exactly the same thing, but he was still focused on microplastics, especially in the inland lakes and ponds. He found that a significant amount of the plastics there were shaped like fibers."

My eyebrows raised. "Really? I would've thought they'd all be micro-beads, since that's the most stable structure!"

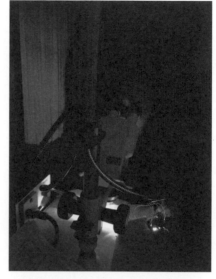

She nodded. "I suppose it's because most of the plastics are made from synthetic textiles like clothing and carpets. Those microplastics get into the water systems as threads, or they might be breaking down from fibrous materials."

The microplastics that have been treated with Nile Red dye are easily differentiated from those that haven't been treated—the ones that have been treated are glowing.

I wasn't quite sure what to make of this information at first. Later, at home, I curled up on the couch next to Andy and looked around the room, feeling sort of restless. My eyes drifted from the purple photo frames to the scratchy, blue blanket, from the white table to the tan dog toy.

That's when another idea hit me.

Most of the different objects I saw in the room were plastics--bright plastics of all sorts of unnatural colors, such as a chartreuse fishing

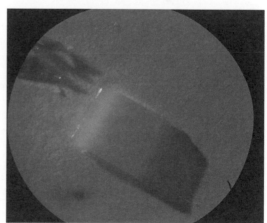

Nile Red (fluorescent) dyed plastics; note how the ends, which are more reactive, are brighter, showing more dye attachment.

lure. I wondered if I could use bright colors, not just infrared, to identify plastics.

If you think about exotic tropical fish like Nemo the clownfish, it might seem that their colors could be the same as some of these synthetic plastic dyes. But what if I combined color information with infrared information? And what if somehow I could look at shape too? Maybe a combination of multiple low-cost systems could have at least the same accuracy as one very expensive identification system. That was really the goal of my project—to create something very low-cost but also efficient.

So, while I first started out looking only at infrared, in the end I decided to use a lot more of the electromagnetic spectrum. It turns out that UV can also be used to cause natural fluorescence in polymers. Yet another way to tell the difference between plastics and non-plastics!

When I added these supplemental systems, the accuracy of my overall detection system increased to 80%. I thought that this would be good for a first-order approach to identifying plastics. If there was a place with a large concentration of microplastics, I should be able to find it.

At first I had to run each program for my different detection systems separately. That was slow, so I decided to make the detection system more autonomous with a website that could access all of the programs with a single click of a button. Building the website took some time, but it was worth it.

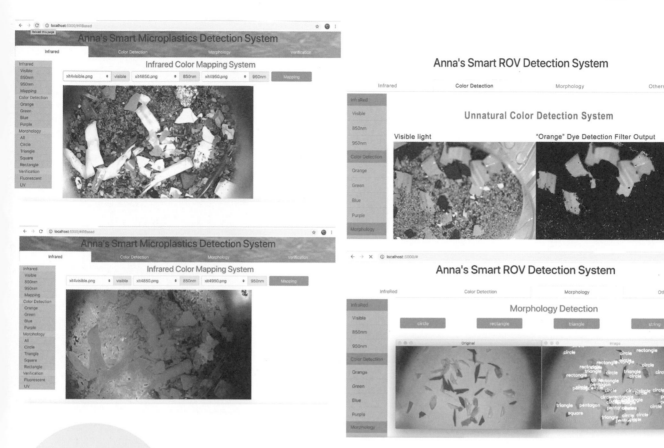

ANNA'S
SCIENCE FAIR TIPS

LOOK BOTH WAYS BEFORE CROSSING DISCIPLINES. If there is any way you can think of to combine your science project with engineering or vice versa, that's the way to go! Cross-disciplinary projects show you can solve problems using different tools across multiple subject areas. In my case, although my project is primarily focused on environmental science, it involves lots of mechanical and electrical engineering as well as computer science too.

Chapter 19

Looking Into The Future

Throughout my journey, I've met people from all walks of life, ranging from students like me or younger to world experts in their field, politicians, teachers, people in entirely different fields of work, and so many more. Whenever the topic of plastic pollution comes up, I find that I always have something to learn. Everyone has a different perspective on life, and therefore, a different perception of a true world problem, along with ideas about how such problems should be addressed.

A couple months ago, I was in line at a restaurant with my family. Right in front of me was a little girl, no older than seven years old.

When it was her family's turn, they ordered tacos. The lady

behind the counter took their order without enthusiasm, and like she had done it millions of times before, plopped a set of plastic forks and knives down on the counter. Just as she was about to turn to my family to take our orders, the little girl spoke up.

"Why'd you give us forks and knives?"

The lady faced the girl and shrugged. "It's my job. It's what we're supposed to do."

The girl shook her head. "We're eating tacos. Why would we need to use forks and knives? It's just a waste, and it's going to kill the fish. Can you take them back?"

The lady stared at her as she took the plastic forks and knives back. I'm sure I was staring too.

What the girl and the lady said really got me thinking—what the lady said was right. She was just following directions, doing the same thing hundreds of times a day, hundreds of days a year, multiplied by hundreds of franchises all around the world.

This mentality, treating everything as cheap and disposable, is so widespread that everyone just falls into it without a second thought. How many times have you been at a party, or at a café, and someone gives you all sorts of utensils that in the end, you really don't need? You probably just threw them away. Not many people would save them—it wouldn't occur to them. Plastics, including single-use plastics, go through such a long journey to get to us, only to be used for a very short period of time, if at all.

I recalled what my teacher told me before I had started. "This problem is so big—how can you solve something you can't fix? It's hopeless."

I thought about that. It's true that this problem is huge, and one that probably won't be fixed for a good many decades. But I can see that I'm not the only person who wants to make a difference. That little girl inspired me.

Whenever I feel like this problem is getting so large, and so out of hand, I think about that little girl, and I remember that there are so many people who care about this problem, and that I'm not alone.

* * *

The night before my first competitive science fair ever—my sixth-grade school science fair—I was an anxious mess. My evening was a blur of hurriedly printing results and graphs, cutting out paper, and slapping it all onto a tri-fold board with double sided sticky tape. At least the glue seemed to hold! When I woke up the next morning, I groggily made my way out of my room. I was still in a sleep-induced haze, and so when I stumbled into the living room, only to see Andy lying down on an explosion of paper, I freaked out.

I sit exhausted in front of my finished science fair display.

"Andy, no!" I shrieked.

I dragged him off of... a pile of paper scraps.

Confused, I looked around. My science fair board was nowhere to be found!

That's when I saw it, propped up against the front door, ready to be taken out. I guess I was so tired the night before that I'd completely forgotten finishing and moving my boards. Andy was free to walk all over the leftover scrap papers without concern.

Still, I couldn't calm down. When I got in my dad's car, I began to tense up. I hugged Andy tightly, reciting my science fair speech to him in the back seat. This was a rare scene—my dad didn't usually allow my dog to ride with me on the way to school, but that day was special. He could tell that I needed to relieve a little tension, and Andy was the perfect way to comfort me.

At school, I could barely focus on any of my classes. My nerves jangled. My entire presentation repeated constantly like a mantra in my head, and I prayed that I wouldn't freeze up and forget everything I had been practicing for weeks.

When the time to present in front of the judges finally came, I felt my voice shake as though I were a solo performer in front of Boston Theater. The whole audience's eyes were on me, scrutinizing my every move. I was terrified that I would make one small mistake and ruin my career.

The judges asked me so many questions that I talked for what seemed like hours. Though I was very prepared and knew my topic well, I'm sure my nervousness showed.

"Wow, this is such a cool project! Are you planning to expand it into more areas?" one judge asked.

"Definitely! There are so many different areas that I'm looking into. One of my goals is to make the machine more autonomous, and spatially map where the microplastics are going to end up, so the clean-up process can be much more efficient. I'm also wondering if I can learn enough about AI to add that in to the project. Maybe I can teach my ROV to identify plastics all by itself."

The judge nodded. "I'm pretty sure you can tackle all that. But you know, some people will question why you're using a big hunk of plastic to go down and clean up plastic trash. What if something were to happen to it, and it failed and sank to the bottom of the ocean floor? Maybe you could create a fail-safe system, so if the ROV were ever to get broken, it could notify someone, so they could try and clean it up."

When it finally came to the awards ceremony, I could feel my heart beating in my chest. All of the honorable mentions were announced... then third place... then second place... Every name that was announced made my breath come faster. Then finally...

"And last but not least... In the first place... Anna Du!"

A breath that I didn't realize I was holding rushed out of me. My parents were clapping in the audience.

That day, on the way home in the car, still reveling in my victory, I thought back to what that judge had said. She wasn't the only judge who had suggested next steps. Many of the judges had mentioned that I should scale my project up, include artificial intelligence, and make it overall more autonomous.

The entire science fair has really helped me in ways I never would have imagined when I started this process. In the beginning, I was just trying to finish a science fair project while doing something that really interested me. But science fair got me doing all sorts of experiments and thinking about how science applied to my everyday life. I like to think I learned how to think like a scientist, constantly designing my experiments and trying to see the world from a science-like point of view.

While we were eating dinner, my mom chatted loudly with

my aunt on the phone. I heard a ping on my phone. James had sent me a poop emoji. That one emoji told me that I had won our months-long argument. I can only hope that he doesn't start calling me Poop now, instead of Butterfly.

I took my judges' advice and got right to work improving my project for the next round of science fairs. I'm still working on it today.

At various science fairs

Left: With Ted Hoff, the inventor of micro processor
Middle: With Mass Science and Engineering Fair (MSEF) Chairperson Barnas Monteith
Right: With Mary Porter from Cabot Corporation, sponsor of MSEF Middle School Fair

Artificial Intelligence & Plastics

The term "AI" can evoke thoughts of evil sentient robots from the future, who travel through time looking to end humanity. However, artificial intelligence is actually more useful as a tool to help people. AI, also known as machine learning, is on the rise in the world of science fairs. More and more, in the past decade, top science fair winners are somehow utilizing AI in their approaches to solve world problems. More than that, AI has become mainstream in our everyday technology, including chatbots and products like Alexa and Siri, as well as fingerprint and handwriting recognition in our phones. Its uses also go far beyond simple communication too. AI has been integrated into surgical tools, self-driving vehicles and analytical equipment in labs and companies.

In recent years, as processing power (including central processing units, graphical processing units, tensor processing units, and more), and storage space have become faster and cheaper, AI tools are becoming possible for a lot of different fields. At the same time, some kinds of data have become more available to the public. Since a lot of AI software has become free and open source, this has made cutting-edge AI possible for students as young as us. For example, my favorite AI platform, Tensorflow (which is actually a collection of a number of different AI tools), was originally developed by Google, but now most of its tools are available for download on Github, by anybody who wants to work on them. Using these tools allows researchers (like me!) to speed up tasks like computer vision, which would otherwise require a lot of hard manual work by humans.

In my case, AI allows for faster identification of possible plastic particles, using image-based data. In the future, my work in AI may involve input from multiple sources, including sensors as well. As opposed to simply using statistics, AI has found a home in the world of science fairs as a means of looking at data interpretation from a different angle, allowing for new ways to explore different subjects, with a low-cost approach, using only math and computers.

Chapter 20

You Can Help Too

The sticky sweet smell of the strawberry wafted through the air in the humid summer afternoon. With a 'splat', I felt something plop onto my sneakers. As I looked down, to my horror, I saw the remains of an overripe strawberry staining my shoe.

"Oops! Sorry about that," my mom said.

I went back to my mission of picking as many strawberries as possible. The strawberries today were just too good to miss. We were at the strawberry farm, and I was having fun, picking the juiciest, reddest strawberries to put in my basket. Being the picky person I am, I would only choose the best out of the best strawberries.

My mom picked up her phone.

I was in the middle of picking another strawberry when my mom gasped.

"Anna—go get your stuff! We're going home immediately!"

I blinked. "Wait... what's going on?"

She was already bustling down the path, and motioned for me to follow her.

"You're getting interviewed by Fox News in an hour!"

"WHAT?"

We hurried off the farm and ran to the car, forgetting our baskets on the way.

"OMG, OMG, OMG!" I kept repeating. I was being interviewed. Wasn't this something that only happened to people like Jennifer Lawrence and Taylor Swift?

What can I do to help the issue of microplastics?

You've probably all heard the saying: reduce, reuse, recycle. Personally, I would also say that another big "R" is research. But, what do these R's actually mean on a practical level? Right now, nearly every town in America (and many throughout the world for that matter) has some form of curbside recycling program. In addition, there are recycling bins at schools, colleges, companies, restaurants and more. Further, many towns have gone a step further and have enacted laws which prevent stores from freely giving away plastic bags, instead charging a small fee for each bag to help cleanup efforts. It would seem that these all add up to a big step in the right direction.

However, while a lot has been done in recent times, there is still a long way to go. The amount of plastics that are dumped annually into the oceans is still on the rise. Regardless of various large-scale ocean cleanup efforts (which cannot even keep up with the annual inflow of plastic pollution, let alone what's already there), and regardless of corporate efforts to use "green"

My mom spent the whole car ride trying to reassure me, "You're going to be fine," "It's all right," and "Anna, you're not dying, please let me focus on the road."

In the end, as soon as the camera turned on me, my mind switched to autopilot and I completely forgot my nerves. Likewise, as soon as the camera turned off, I started freaking out again, worried that I had somehow messed something up.

It's been a couple of months since then. I'm really motivated to keep working on my project. I've been finding out a lot about machine learning and AI, and I'm starting to give my computer loads of examples and data so it can start teaching itself how to identify plastic particles. I've been thinking that perhaps, in the

biodegradable plastic alternatives in many consumer products, the problem continues to grow larger over time. That makes the matter of cleaning up microplastics even more difficult.

The problem with many of these efforts is that there is just such an overwhelmingly large amount of single use plastics in our daily lives. I mean, think about how many times you've gone to a café or a fast food restaurant and were given a plastic container and plastic cutlery, only to use it for a few minutes. Or, not even use them at all. These plastics have such an incredibly short useful lifetime, but they continue to live on in landfills, forests, beaches and oceans for generations. The absolute best way to prevent this problem from growing is prevention. If we all, especially in our generation, consciously agree to use fewer single-use plastics in our daily lives (or eliminate them altogether) that may be the only way to prevent a future riddled with microplastics. And of course, the more we collaborate together around the planet and do research on the best ways to clean these plastics up without harming the living members of our global environment, the closer we can get to a pollution-free future.

future, I could have a whole swarm of ROVs, a whole army out in the ocean, searching for microplastics, and potentially even cleaning them up! Meantime, I've been interviewed a lot more times, and I've even had to give talks to large groups of people. The nerves never truly go away, but they've become more manageable. I've slowly started to look forward to the next interview,

not because I'm getting more famous, or because my project is gaining attention, but because more people are now aware of the issue of microplastics pollution. This is one of the best parts of my recent media attention— it allows me to spread the message to places that I never knew possible. Now, more people know about this problem and are willing to dedicate time to try and help solve it.

Working on a real engineering problem has given me a chance to express my ideas and feel a sense of accomplishment that regular school classes can't match. Experiencing that has reinforced my interest in one day becoming an engineer. It has also made me think that it's possible to tackle almost any problem.

One day, my friend Alissa asked me, "Hey, Anna, do you know if I can recycle this?"

I felt like that one question brightened up my whole day. Alissa's question meant some of my friends were now ready to join me to change their lifestyles—even a little bit.

The problem of microplastics pollution in the ocean is similar to a lot of other issues that are potentially devastating to our lives. In order to make a dent in the problem, we need to start doing something now, before it reaches the point of no return. But this doesn't mean everybody has to dedicate their lives to patrolling the beach or traveling the ocean to clean up plastics. Right now, most of the 5 trillion metric tons of plastics in the ocean are the plastics that we use in our daily lives. Each of us can make a dent in the pile of trash that goes out our door.

One idea I've started thinking about is this: What if people had their own, personal recycling facilities in their own homes? Right now, plastic numbers 3-7 are usually all sent to a landfill. But if people could somehow recycle at home, we could solve the problem of both single-use plastics and plastics that people think they're recycling when they're really getting dumped in landfills.

Personally, I think a ramped-up recycling and manufacturing plan would also be a great way for communities to get together—especially young people—to work on projects that combine science, engineering, community service and education. This is an idea I want to keep working on—and maybe you could too.

But to make a difference, you don't have to do home recycling. There is a much simpler solution—upcycling. Upcycling is where one object that no longer has any use is remade into something that is useful, and sometimes beautiful as well. In the 1930s-40s, following the Great Depression, many families in the US were living in poverty. People repurposed objects as much as possible. They made buckets from tires, or dining room tables from broken doors.

If we want to do something to try and help solve a massive problem like microplastics pollution in the ocean, we can't just tackle it full on. Instead, we need to break it into manageable pieces, like recycling, upcycling, and reducing our use of plastics. The same goes for cleanup solutions. So with my project, instead of finding a way to clean up plastics directly, I'm first looking for a way to locate and detect the plastics in the ocean, so cleanup systems won't have to go through the entire ocean blindly sucking in everything they brush against. Instead, they will know exactly how to home in on the places with the most plastics.

Many young people in America and other countries have great ideas that just might help the world. I know I'm lucky that my family, mentors, and teachers have been so supportive. One thing I've found is that when you ask for help and show that you're working hard on a good idea, many older people will be willing to give you time and advice.

More and more opportunities present themselves for students my age to learn about major problems facing the world. Public television networks and other informative organizations communicate these concepts in a way that is understandable to young students, and that inspires us to do something to help. We all have dreams of creating or becoming something much bigger than ourselves, whether it's to cure disease, to carry out ground-breaking research, or to engineer new approaches to some of the world's biggest problems.

This was a story about my dream, and how I turned it into a reality. Each and every one of us has our own dream. We have the ability to make it a reality too.

ANNA'S
SCIENCE FAIR TIPS

No matter whether you win or lose, believe it or not, your science fair experience is sure to be fun—and you can learn a lot along the way!

ACTIVITIES:

BREAKING DOWN

Microplastics break down as they enter the ocean, but the smaller a piece gets, the harder it is to break down, especially when it becomes circular. Microbeads are among the hardest substances for the ocean to break down — simply because of their shape! Spheres are the most stable shape compared to everything else — for example, if you had a sphere and a right rectangular prism, what do you think is harder to break in half? Here, you can try this experiment.

Materials:

· just a pencil! :)

Instructions

1. First, make sure the pencil you're using isn't anyone else's. We don't want someone to not get their homework done just for this one experiment!
2. Try to break this pencil in half.
3. Try it again.
4. And again.
5. How many times can you break it in half? And what do you notice?

Breaking a pencil

MAGIC DENSITY BOTTLE

One of the original ideas I had for identifying microplastics was to look at the density of the object. I quickly wrote that idea out, because it was too complicated with every different type of plastic having a different density. However, that still doesn't stop density from being a good identifier of different, specific objects. This activity allows you to see why.

Density bottle

Materials:
- a small bottle
- two different types of beads
- isopropyl alcohol
- water
- salt
- food dye (optional)

Instructions:
1. Fill the bottle halfway up with water. Add salt to the water. Then, if you want to, put a few drops of food dye in the water.
2. Stir the saltwater solution until all the salt inside has dissolved.
3. Fill the rest of the bottle up with isopropyl alcohol.
4. Place the two types of beads inside.

5. Seal off the bottle.

6. Shake the bottle, and watch what happens!

OCEAN SIMULATION MACHINE

In order to simulate the effects of plastics underwater, I created something like this. Plastics go through a lot of abrasion in the ocean, whether it's from the rolling waves, or other materials in the ocean grinding on them. However, this can also be used to create realistic looking sea glass as well.

Ocean simulation machine

Materials:
- a big motor
- cardboard box
- tape
- zip-tie
- sand
- glass
- shells (optional)
- 2 old water bottles
- water

Instructions:

1. Cut a hole in the side of a cardboard box which fits the size of the large motor snugly.

2. Get one of the water bottles and cut it in half. Recycle the side that has the mouthpiece.

3. Cut the half of the water bottle that wasn't recycled downwards, three fourths of the way to the bottom.

4. Connect the halved water bottle to the motor.

5. Take the untouched water bottle, and fill it with sand,

glass, and shells. Fill it up part of the way with water.

6. Attach the zipline on, making sure to leave enough room so later, when you put on the water bottle, it will fit.

7. Place the filled water bottle inside the halved one, making sure it's in snugly.

8. Loop the zip tie around the water bottle.

9. Turn the motor on, and wait! Depending on how abraded you want your objects to be, you can keep it going from a week to months.

THE TEMPERATURE OF THE RAINBOW

This experiment is to show you that beyond what we can see of the rainbow, there are different parts of the electromagnetic spectrum as well. In my book, Ed and I talked about how different parts of the rainbow would have different temperatures — even the parts that we can't see!

Materials:

- prism
- cardboard box
- white paper
- four thermometers
- scissors

NASA rainbow test

Instructions:

1. Take the cardboard box, and place the white sheet of paper in it.

2. Cut a hole in the top of the box that can fit the prism in securely.

3. Place the cardboard box somewhere where a bright light can filter through the prism — preferably outside. You should see a rainbow appear.

4. Place one of the thermometers on the bottom of the paper, one on the orange, one on the blue, and one right outside the purple.

5. Record the temperatures. See what happens!

BUILD YOUR OWN RELAY

In order to give my motors more power, and not damage other electronics, I used a relay to separate them into two different systems. There are different ways relays can work—some are based on detecting light, but this one is based on magnetism.

Materials:
- 5 alligator clips
- two batteries
- cardboard scraps
- strip of metal
- screw
- wire
- buzzer/light/something to visualize that the system is working

Instructions:
1. Make a stand out of cardboard in the shape of an L and place the screw in the bottom of it.

2. Wrap a wire around the screw, making sure to leave both ends out

3. Connect the first alligator clip to the top of the wire
   a. Connect the other side to the first battery.

4. Connect the metal scrap to the top of the ⊏ to make a [shape.

5. Connect the second alligator clip to the metal scrap

    a. connect the other side to the positive of the second battery

6. Connect the third alligator clip to the screw

7. Connect the other side to the positive side of the buzzer

    a. Connect the fourth alligator clip to the negative side of the second battery

8. Connect the other side to the negative side of the buzzer

    a. Connect the second alligator clip to the bottom side of the wire.

9. You should see the metal scrap come down to touch the screw, completing the circuit, and the buzzer should go off.

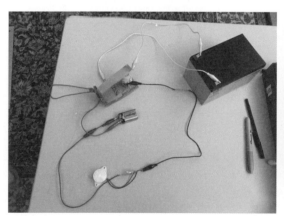

Relay experiment

ETCH-A-CIRCUIT

For my project, I etched my own design on a copper-clad board in order to create my circuit. You can do the same thing too! But you don't have to create a circuit—using this method, you can etch whatever you want!

Materials:

- sodium hydroxide
- ferric chloride
- copper-clad board
- laminator
- light-sensitive paper
- sharpie or transparent sheet
- paintbrush
- gloves

Instructions:

1. Place the light-sensitive paper on top of the copper-clad board.
2. Laminate them together.
3. Either use sharpie, or use a transparent sheet of paper, and draw/print your design backwards.

    a. If you were using a transparent sheet of paper, attach it to the board with tape.

4. Place it in the sun for a few hours.
5. Dip the board in sodium hydroxide. Make sure to protect your skin with gloves from this point on!
6. Wash the board off.
7. Dip the board in ferric chloride.
8. Slowly remove the parts which weren't exposed to the sun, and not bonded to the board, with a paintbrush.
9. Wash the board off again. Ta da!! You've just etched your own pattern in copper.

BIBLIOGRAPHY

https://www.scientificamerican.com/article/from-fish-to-humans-a-microplastic-invasion-may-be-taking-a-toll/

https://blog.frontiersin.org/2018/02/21/marine-science-plastic-pollution-ocean-atlantic-fish/

https://www.ecowatch.com/table-salt-microplastics-2613395969.html

https://www.plasticsmakeitpossible.com/about-plastics/types-of-plastics/what-are-plastics/

https://www.newscientist.com/article/mg13918823-500-technology-infrared-makes-light-work-of-sorting-plastics/

http://coolcosmos.ipac.caltech.edu/cosmic_classroom/classroom_activities/herschel_example.html

http://coolcosmos.ipac.caltech.edu/cosmic_games/spectra/makeGrating.html

https://www.nasa.gov/centers/jpl/education/wise-20091123.html

https://greentumble.com/how-is-plastic-recycled-step-by-step/

IMAGE CREDITS

ABOUT THE AUTHOR

Anna Du is thirteen years old and she's a big fan of both science and engineering. Through her explorations of beaches, she developed a strong appreciation for the ocean and marine life. For the past several years, she has focused on the globally increasing widespread microplastic pollution. Her invention is an underwater ROV, which uses infrared combined with artificial intelligence to identify and spatially map regions of microplastic accumulation. She has been named as one of the top ten young scientists by 3M-Discovery channel, as well as one of the top 30 students in the nation by the Broadcom Masters Program for 2018 and 2019.

Me and Rachel Carson in Woods Hole, Massachusettes